The Urban Circulation Noose

A New Collection By Duxbury Press.

THE MAN-ENVIRONMENT SYSTEM IN THE LATE TWENTIETH CENTURY

General Editor
WILLIAM L. THOMAS
California State University, Hayward

The Food and People Dilemma	*Georg A. Borgstrom*
Human Geography in a Shrinking World: The Geography of Alternative Futures	*Ronald Abler, Donald Janelle, Allen Philbrick and John Sommer (Eds.)*
The Urban Circulation Noose	*James O. Wheeler*
Your Land or Your Life: Indian Lands in Modern America	*John Q. Ressler*
Remote Sensing: A Broader View of the Man-Environment System	*Robert D. Rudd*

THE URBAN CIRCULATION NOOSE

JAMES O. WHEELER
University of Georgia

DUXBURY PRESS
North Scituate, Massachusetts
A Division of Wadsworth
Publishing Company, Inc.
Belmont, California

Duxbury Press
A Division of Wadsworth Publishing Company, Inc.

ISBN-0-87872-056-1

L. C. Cat. Card No. 73-89887
Printed in the United States of America
1   2   3   4   5   6   7   8   9   10   —   76   75   74

Contents

Editor's Foreword

Geography's renaissance, during the past two decades, has given rise to thought deserving of a wider audience. The discipline has adopted a dynamic, problem-solving attitude; it has incorporated behavioral science research into its methodology; it uses more rigorous methods of analysis; and it has given renewed emphasis to the tradition of man as a manager of his total environment: a problem-creater and a problem-solver. It is the purpose of the series "The Man-Environment System in the Late 20th Century" to provide a forum through which the new ideas and syntheses in geography may quickly reach the broadest possible audience.

Each volume in this series will cover a topic of social relevance that currently occupies one of the frontiers of multi-disciplinary research and whose findings should beneficially widen the intellectual horizons of an informed public. The creative thinkers, researchers, and scholars selected as authors have been challenged to express themselves with style, liveliness, apt examples, and humor. It is my hope, as editor of the series, that every volume will be the equivalent of an integrated set of seven or eight lectures given by the author on a topic that is close to his heart.

Dr. James O. Wheeler is Professor of Geography at the University of Georgia. He received his Ph.D. in Geography from Indiana University in 1966 and has been a faculty member at Ohio State, Western Michigan, and Michigan State Universities. The present volume is the culmination of seven years of research and brings together his thoughts expressed in 21 articles published in 15 different journals in the United States, Sweden, Netherlands, and India. Wheeler has explored a wide spectrum of the research literature on transportation, communication, social research, and urban planning and has brought it together in an innovative way. He demonstrates how circulation processes (in movement or flow of ideas, goods, and people via transportation and communication) form an integral part of our urban system and interlink with a multitude of social problems in our cities. The solution to many of our current urban problems lies in a greater awareness of the social effects of *The Urban Circulation Noose.*

WILLIAM L. THOMAS

Preface

This short book contains a series of essays on the role of transportation and communication in the changing social conditions of our growing metropolitan areas. The implications are broad, since social change affects all of us; since we all intimately participate in circulation, i.e., transportation and communications; and since most of us live in or near metropolitan areas. The topic treated here is vital because current indications are that changes in our urban systems are accelerating, but not necessarily toward resolution of existing social conflicts and problems. The fundamental and encompassing role of urban circulation as it interacts with changing social issues is too little recognized and appreciated by both the interested layman and the urban and transportation policy planner. It is therefore the purpose of this book to provide insight into some of the more critical social, and hence human, implications of urban transportation and communications.

Three themes are interwoven into these essays. One is the role of circulation as it lays the basis for the spatial organization of people and their activities in urban areas. A second is spatial organization as it influences social organization. Third are the transportation and communication systems and their evolution as they precipitate social stress.

The book is divided into eight chapters. The first demonstrates the interdependence between movement space in the urban area and some of the most basic problems facing the burgeoning metropolis. In order to understand the overall problems of urban living, one must have specific insight into the circulation system which carries the city's lifeblood and is the metropolitan pulse. Chapter 2 examines human social movement from place to place in the city and the opportunities and nature of social interaction. One of the central factors affecting social contact is place of residence, which in turn is linked to place of work. Chapter 3 treats the residential location decision and the associated problems of getting to work. Since the journey to work is especially difficult for many blacks living in our urban ghettos, Chapter 4 focuses directly on this issue and explores the conflicts involved in freeway penetration into black ghettos.

The next chapter takes up the increasingly important role communication is playing in urban society, particularly for industrial firms. As the cost of communication declines relative to other costs and as new electronic technology expands possibilities for information handling, cities are being affected as fundamentally as they were by the railroad in the 19th century or the automobile in this century. A variety of implications of the communication revolution are discussed in Chapter 6, with special reference to social considerations in urban transport policy. In Chapter 7, the urban transportation planning process is described within the context of the future urban society, and some comments are offered on the role of circulation in planning and public policy. The last chapter, tying the seven essays together, views circulation as a vital part of the changing urban system.

This book should appeal to a wide variety of readers, from students of transportation, urban planning, business administration and policy, marketing, and political science to students of sociology and geography, as well as to the interested layman. It is written to be understood by everyone concerned with urban living, including those in positions of public policy decision making. The book, although written by a geographer and including a geographic or spatial perspective, seeks to avoid much of the confusing jargon and confining reliance on rigid academic boundaries so often encountered in publications designed for restricted professional consumption. It is hoped that the book will have a practical value and offer insight to the socially responsible person.

A long list of individuals have contributed to the formulation of this book, both directly and indirectly, wittingly and unwittingly. My primary initial stimulation in the field of transportation geography came from Robert N. Taaffe and Edward J. Taaffe, whose quiet inspiration has sustained me over the years.

James O. Wheeler

Athens, Georgia
July, 1973

Chapter 1

The Role of Circulation
in Urban Problems

Throughout man's history the transportation of goods, information, and himself has been a principal frustration. With every advance in conveyance and communication, man has reached new levels of frustration, as his desires for mobility always exceeded his transport achievements. Each of man's transportation revolutions so changed his society that further transport innovation was deemed a necessity to the continual functioning of that society. And yet, of course, each improvement in transportation and communication technology has compelled further change in society itself. A circular system has thus been set into motion, change being induced simply by attempts to sustain the system.

From man's very beginnings a principal source of power in transportation has been human muscle. For unnumbered ages man could move himself only where his own legs would carry him, could transport burdens only with his own weak back, and could communicate only within the limited range of his voice. By dragging materials over the ground, or by putting rollers or wheels under them to reduce friction, man was able to move goods in small bulk. By applying his muscle to water craft, he likewise could transport small loads over short distances. To his own muscles, he added those of animals and the force of the winds to multiply many times the range of his movement and the size of his loads. The total impact on society of the use of animal power in locomotion was profound. But after the subjugation of animals for land transport followed most of man's historic era on this earth, during which no significant improvement in transport efficiency occurred:

> *And the weighty fact is that this immense and complex*
> *organism, with all its accumulations of wealth and wisdom, its*
> *diversified employments, its agriculture, manufacturers,*
> *business affairs, financial systems, commercial and political*
> *relations, civil and social order — its very life and potency — was*
> *not only fitted to but dependent upon means of transportation*
> *which, as respects their expense, speed and capacity, had not es-*
> *sentially altered since the earliest tribes began to barter!*[1]

But with the development of steam power for locomotion, both over water and land, not yet two centuries ago, man felt himself suddenly unchained from the oppression of distance which had placed such high hurdles in the path of civilization. One writer at the turn of the present century exclaimed about the far-reaching effect of steam driven conveyances, unaware of the even greater changes about to occur around him in motorized movement:

> *No other triumph over the forces of nature compares with*
> *this in its influence upon human environment. It has directly*
> *and powerfully affected the direction and volume of commercial*
> *currents, the location and movements of population, the oc-*
> *cupations and pursuits in which the masses of men are engaged,*
> *the division of labor, the conditions under which wealth is ac-*
> *cumulated, the social and industrial habits of the world, all the*
> *surroundings and characteristics of the associate life of today.*
> *The world has seen no change so sudden and so amazing.*[2]

And yet, within the last fifty years, changes of even greater magnitude in transportation and communication have occurred with snowballing effect.

What ocean-going vessels did for the growth and dominance of port cities, the railroad did for inland cities, at the same time maintaining the role of those port cities favorably connected by rail to the interior. A pattern of urbanism followed at strategic locations on the railroad network. Yet within cities internal movement did not change noticeably, and it was the motor vehicle, self-propelled by the internal combustion engine, that was largely to alter the configuration of locations and the lifestyles within the urban areas. Moreover, the once mighty railroads of the nineteenth and early twentieth centuries, with the competition from motorized transport, fell into eclipse as a means of transporting people and high value goods.

While the railroad had a profound influence on differential growth, its effect was highly structured and dependent upon access to and position on the rail network. By contrast, motorized vehicles could travel nearly everywhere on the dense and rapidly extended system of roads and streets. During the early part of this century the railway's impact was felt regionally, whereas the automobile and truck exerted primarily a local influence. Later, especially after World War II, highway movement replaced the railroad in determining regional impact and city growth. Thus, from its beginnings highway movement has been intimately linked with urban transportation, supplemented in part by mass transport and by muscle power, the oldest form of movement. This highway transport has brought unparalleled social and economic change to the city. Moreover, highway transport has evolved through almost yearly, and hence nearly imperceptible, improvements both in vehicles and roadways.

Of all places on the earth, it is the cities where the transportation needs are most critical, where the movement of goods and people is most intensified, and where the flows of information reach their highest and most complexly interwoven patterns. Essentially, modern cities exist to facilitate man's mobility. Cities provide a concentration of people and activities such that movement and communication among them may be achieved at a low overall cost. In this regard, the city is man's most complicated but, at the same time, efficient system yet devised to communicate and interact over space. Each urban individual has, with a minimum of expended effort, access to the most astronomical and far-reaching set of communication sources and variety of activities ever before experienced by mankind. This transportation and communication service is the single most important reason that people live in cities. Indeed, circulation in the modern city has come to occupy such a central and fundamental role in the functional operation of urban affairs that it is necessarily bound up both with the present problems and future potentialities of city life.

Change as an Urban Problem

The rapid evolution in transportation stemming from the motor revolution has quickened the pace of change in the city. The history of urbanization in the twentieth century has been a history of urban change, and a survey of the growing urban problems of the modern city is a survey of difficulties created by change. Whether the problems center on housing conditions, racial segregation, administrative fragmentation, crime, crowded schools, unemployment, pollution, or traffic congestion and accidents, they are all the products of change having occurred too rapidly for adjustment processes to keep up. Each of these problems is related, some directly and others indirectly, to the essential transportation and communication function for which cities exist.

The very nature of the city is changing, much of it in response both to transportation improvements and to traffic congestion. The rapid rate of this change confuses the observer wishing to understand urban problems and the nature of city life. There are many factors involved in a single problem. Which are the primary ones? Which are related to the cause and which to the consequences? Even the perception of what constitutes an urban problem is dependent upon one's comprehension of how the city works or should work. The speed of change is bewildering, and yet planning and policy decisions must be made daily. Clearly, an understanding of the modern city demands an understanding of the process of change, a casting away of old images of the city, and fresh analyses of new relationships as they alter the urban structure.

If the rate of urban change could somehow be slowed and the urban complex allowed to stabilize, most of the problems could be solved, or at least attacked. Housing availability could be more readily adjusted to housing needs, downtown commercial decline could be slowed or reversed if the city simply quit growing outward so quickly, and transport demands could be more easily translated to transport facilities if traffic would not continue to increase at such an unbelievably rapid rate.

There seems to be no indication, however, that urban growth and change will be slowed. In fact, this country has seen a continual expansion of urbanism, from 1790 when only four percent of the population lived in cities, to 1918 — the year one-half the people were first classified as urban — to the present time when three-quarters of the U. S. population lives in metropolitan systems. This urbanization has gone hand-in-hand with industrialization in particular and technology in general; both have been attracted to and concentrated in cities. Despite its many problems and deficiencies, the city remains a favored place to live both for its social and economic advantages. It is paradoxical that these advantages would be even more widely perceived if the present disadvantages of city life were not quite so great. It is the advantage of urban living, recognized by increasing numbers, that causes the urban change, confusion, and congestion.

Let us examine some relationships between urban change, circulation, and selected metropolitan social problems. It is the intent of these introductory pages to set the stage for the issues taken up in the following chapters. Specifically, two overriding urban themes are outlined in this chapter to illustrate the role of transportation in metropolitan problems. These are, first, the geographical relationships between urban housing and transportation and, second, traffic and communication congestion. These two themes form a foundation for the subsequent chapters and bring into focus two of the most troublesome social aspects of urban circulation. Traffic congestion, of course, is a direct result of transporta-

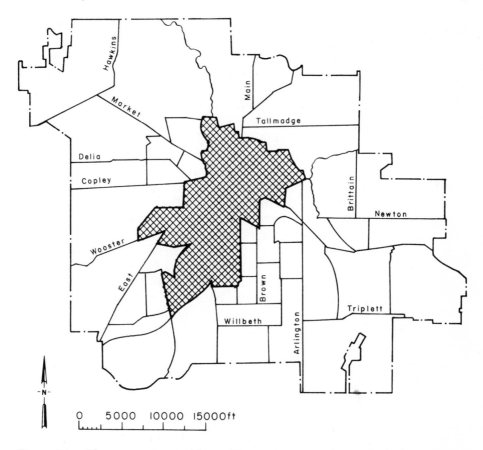

Figure 1.1: The poverty area in Akron, Ohio, encompasses the older housing districts in the center of the city, as well as having a sectoral effect toward the southeast.

tion problems, whereas housing patterns in a city, like many other problems, are tied to transportation in less obvious ways. Communication foul-ups and bottlenecks present a most serious but infrequently recognized issue in urban living.

Housing and Transportation

The old saw that "a house is not a home" aptly describes the essential condition of housing for growing numbers of urban residents: there are too many people living in substandard structures in the city. For these people, a desire for improved housing, however, is not matched by an ability to afford a better structure. Stated otherwise, there is insufficient low cost housing of adequate quality available in the urban area.

Low quality housing tends to be geographically concentrated in the city, particularly within the older sections near the downtown. Moreover, the old and run-down housing in these areas, consisting of ramshackle apartments, tenements, and large multi-family houses once the grand homes of the urban elite, accommodates the highest population densities anywhere in the city. Here live the urban poor of all types, the helpless and hopeless, bitter and belligerent, young and old, white and black. Let us consider how transportation is related to the crowded living of the urban poor in the decaying heart of the modern city (Figure 1.1).

It seems at first impossible that the poor live on the most expensive land in the city and that the suburban rich occupy the least costly land, just recently transferred from agricultural use. Nevertheless, such is the pattern of land values, decreasing irregularly the farther one goes from the downtown business district. The geographical distribution of population density also follows a very similar decline away from downtown, having its highest densities in the old and run-down areas adjacent to downtown and having its lowest densities at the periphery where city merges into countryside. A low-income household typically lives on some of the most expensive land, but because of high density living, occupies only a very small living space; in contrast, the high-income family consumes a large amount of relatively inexpensive land. The basic reason for the association of population concentration and land values is transportation accessibility.[3]

A household with a given amount of income has several choices in disposing of it. These decisions will be made in order to achieve a particular level of satisfaction. How a household chooses to spend money may depend on many things, such as the number of people in the family, preferences for entertainment, and even personality factors. However, these influences on spending will exist wherever the household lives in the city. Thus the only two major expenditures which will vary with the location of the household are rent for housing and transportation costs. The latter cost of course depends on the household's accessibility to the various points within the city, such as workplace, shopping facilities, and other business establishments. For any particular household, there will be a logical tendency to trade off the amount one is willing to pay for housing with the amount one is willing to pay for transportation.

Even if all households had the same income, as well as similar preferences for housing, the per unit price of housing would have to decrease away from downtown. At a greater distance from the city center, one incurs higher transportation costs, as one would generally be located farther from the major activities in the city. With constant income and high cost of movement, less money will be left over for housing the greater the distance from the center of the city, the location which has the highest concentration of activities. Nevertheless, this discussion still does not explain the phenomenon of the rich living on the cheapest land.

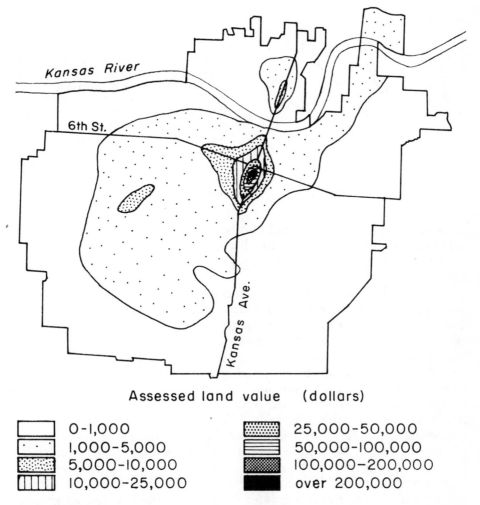

Assessed land value (dollars)

0-1,000		25,000-50,000
1,000-5,000		50,000-100,000
5,000-10,000		100,000-200,000
10,000-25,000		over 200,000

Figure 1.2: Assessed land values in Topeka, Kansas, 1954 - 1959. Note the rapid decline in land values away from the center of the city. Taken from Duane Knos, *The Distribution of Land Values in Topeka* (Kansas: University of Kansas, Bureau of Business and Economic Research, 1962).

Consider the plight of a low-income household. The family cannot afford the luxury of a high level of mobility. Furthermore, the household can afford only a small unit of housing. These two constraints, mobility and housing, restrict the household to a residential location near the center of the city where transportation costs are relatively low. At the same time, such a residential location, being highly accessible, must compete with commercial and industrial establishments also desirous of access. The value of the land, owing to its accessibility, is high, and the only way in which residential land use can successfully compete is by in-

Figure 1.3: The changing relationship between transportation cost and housing site quality for three time periods, T¹, T², T³. Transportation costs increase for all three periods away from the center of the city, C. However, in the most recent time period, T³, moving farther from the center of the city to obtain better housing quality entails only a modest increase in transportation cost, compared to earlier time periods.

creasing the density of household units. Hence, a low-income family, unable to afford mobility, locates in a highly accessible area, consumes only a small amount of land, but pays a high rent per unit of that land (Figure 1.2).

A high-income family, in contrast, is free to reside wherever it wishes in the city. Not restricted by the costs of overcoming distance and desiring a larger amount of living space, such a household normally locates in a lower density suburban area. The family is able to afford the higher transportation cost as well as more housing and space. The most desirable locations in a city with highly mobile inhabitants are therefore in the suburban area. Households, in fact, purchase two separate kinds of commodities when they select a residence. They pay for both the location and the site characteristics. The former may be measured in transportation dollars, accessibility, or the commuting time spent on the journey to work, whereas the site has such features as lot size, landscaping, trees and shrubbery, slope, and general quality of neighborhood. The high-income household, wanting high quality site amenities, is simply willing and able to travel a greater distance to obtain a desired site.

The general geographical pattern of housing in cities is thus related to transportation costs. In Figure 1.3, the relationship between transportation and housing site quality is described as it has changed over three periods of time (t¹, t², and t³). Point C in the diagram is the center of the city. Transport costs increase with distance from this center. The quality of housing sites also is shown to increase away from point C. Since cities have historically advanced over the landscape like a ripple in a pool from a thrown rock, the older housing is found nearer the downtown, with the newer homes at the edge of the growing city. During the period of horse-drawn vehicles (t¹), the cost of transport was extremely high relative to the cost of housing. The purchase of an additional hypothetical unit of housing quality would produce a steep increase in

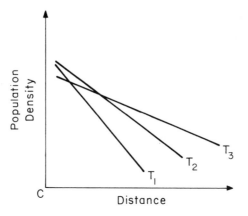

Figure 1.4: The decline in population density with distance from center of city, C, is most rapid in the first time period, T^1. At T^3, the decline is not only less steep but also the population has spread out farther away from the city center, while the population near the center of the city has had an absolute decline.

transportation costs. Stated otherwise, there was rather little difference in housing site amenities within the youthful city, but there were big differences in transport costs depending on location within the city. As transport technology improved in the next period (t^2), bringing about higher levels of mobility and a reduction in cost, the purchase of that additional hypothetical unit of housing quality meant a smaller transport increase. Finally, at the present time (t^3), only a very small increase in transportation costs is brought about by moving farther from the city center to obtain an additional unit of housing quality. The social structure of urban housing has thus changed from the rich living near the center during the period of high transport costs to the rich living at the city's edge during the present period of high mass mobility. With improved transportation, the most desirable living space has changed from an innercity to a suburban location.

Improved transportation has helped speed up the process of innercity housing decay. Figure 1.4 shows the overall population changes that have occurred in the three time periods noted above. In the first period (t^1), population density decreased with distance from C, the city center, because of the difficulty in overcoming distance. Examination of the density decline in the second period (t^2) indicates a faster rate of growth in the suburban area than in the innercity. In period three (t^3), mobility has reached such a high level that not only has the suburban growth increased at a faster rate but also the city has grown several miles out into the formerly agricultural landscape. At the same time, the population of the innercity has experienced an absolute numerical decline. In the earlier years of suburbanization, i. e., migration of households from the innercity to the suburbs, the migration was highly selective and primarily included those in the higher socioeconomic levels. As transport costs continued to fall, those in the middle of the socioeconomic ladder also began to select suburban residential locations. The suburbs, once associated almost exclusively with high-income households, are now much more mixed, although residential suburbs continue to have concentrations of households by socioeconomic status.

In the meantime the innercity has become a less and less prestigious residential location. Most of the rich have moved out. So too have many of the middle-income families, especially if they have children. Segregated minorities, particularly blacks, have not been able to participate in the suburbanization characterizing much of the white population. Indeed, the presence of low-income blacks in the innercity (given the realities of white racism) has spurred on the white exodus to the suburbs. Innercity families are increasingly trapped in the declining center because of racial discrimination, low income, old age, or a combination of these reasons.

The quality of housing in the innercity has been allowed to decline as well. With the drop in purchasing power resulting from migration to the suburbs of high-income families, the commercial establishments of the innercity began to feel the financial pinch. Commercial suburbanization thus began in an effort to follow the migrating purchasing power. Lower retail profits in the innercity meant that less money was available to renovate store fronts and generally maintain the normal quality of appearance. The worsening appearance of commercial areas induced additional migration to the suburbs, leading in turn to further commercial blight and decay. A downward cycle of deterioration set in, with commercial blight successively bringing about deteriorating housing followed by more commercial decay.

No countervailing process has operated to maintain residential quality. The fine mansions and homes of the rich were converted into multiple-family units of the poor. Each year these structures became older and more in need of repair. Maintenance and renewal, however, meant higher taxes, and the taxation system "punished" property owners who maintained their buildings. Given the prevailing social attitude toward the innercity, there was little incentive to invest in housing improvement. A result of the lowered tax base was a reduction in governmental services. Moreover, a landowner could realize a sizable profit from what had come to be a slum dwelling by packing families into old houses or dilapidated apartment buildings. The cost of renovation became out of balance with the additional profit to be realized from remodeling, and a full-fledged slum resulted. Much of the housing of our present-day innercities is in various stages of such slum development.

In this indirect sense, therefore, transportation improvements have contributed significantly to the creation of our innercity slums. In a way surely unanticipated by the early transport innovators, a fundamental change in the entire structure, function, and appearance of the city was set into motion. The changes produced by transport have been too fast for the city to adjust adequately to the housing needs of all its citizens. However, the housing problems of the modern city represent only one of a long list of difficulties tied to urban change and to transportation considerations. Another and related problem is traffic and communication congestion, a direct result of increased levels of personal mobility and of the information explosion.

Congestion

Traffic congestion results simply from competition for space and the desires of large numbers of people to reach favored locations at particular times of the day. Traffic snarls occur predictably whenever the volume of traffic exceeds the capacity of the urban street and freeway network.

Each city street has its own capacity, measured in the number of vehicles per hour able to pass a point at the legal limit of speed. When more automobiles attempt to use a street segment or an intersection than can be accommodated, congestion not only results at that particular location but also spreads along other streets and intersections, as traffic backs up over an ever-widening area. A single bottleneck, even during nonrush hours, may affect traffic flow over a sizable section of the city, as the diverted traffic may increase flow volume beyond capacity on adjacent streets and intersections. During the rush hour, when travel needs reach their highest level, traffic in fact creeps more slowly than at any other time, and the urban area becomes virtually paralyzed when its greatest energy is released.

In this regard, urban transportation may be viewed as a system seeking an equilibrium with itself. When out of balance, transportation adversely affects the larger urban system of which it is a part. The transportation arteries of the city may be likened to the arteries of the human body, and movements within the urban corpus may be compared to blood. The urban circulatory system transports and directs the energy that is essential to the city's life, carries much of the waste and garbage generated by daily living, and maintains the pace at which the city functions. Urban circulation, from its arterials to its alleys, connects places separated by distance, allows messages, goods, and people to travel from any place to any other place in urban space. An area of the city suddenly cut off from its transportation ties could not long survive, just as a body organ dies when deprived of the flow of blood. Likewise, as a blood clot may create swelling, or vascular congestion, so too does traffic volume reach intolerable pressures and restrict the capacity for movement, producing a daily swell that curtails the efficiency of the entire city. As an organism the city indeed is ill. Urban wastes build up to choke and

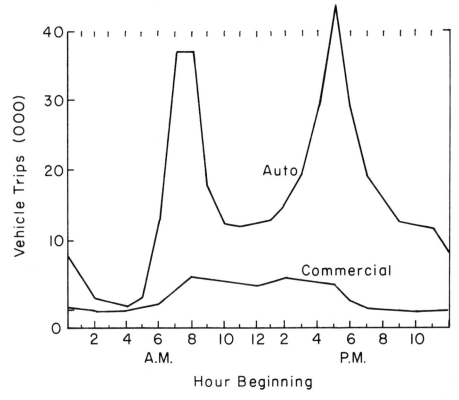

Figure 1.5: Survey counts of auto and commercial vehicle trips by hour of day in Pittsburgh. Note the morning and afternoon peaks. Taken from *Pittsburgh Area Transportation Study*, Vol. 1, Study Findings, 1961.

benumb hopeless inhabitants. Communication circuits overload and essential information becomes lost, wasted, or distorted. No living organism could survive with its circulatory requirements so hopelessly out of balance.

Traffic volume for the city as a whole typically exceeds capacity from approximately 7:00 to 9:00 a.m. and from 4:00 to 6:00 p.m., depending on the specific city (Figure 1.5). These two peak periods result largely from individuals going to and coming from work and school. However, the capacity of most streets is not reached at any other time of day; during the late evening and early morning hours the system is particularly underused.

Why does this pattern of traffic pile-ups occur? The city performs its work as a city by concentrating a great many people into relatively small spaces. The nature of industrial technology is such that workers must be brought into close spatial proximity to carry out the manufacturing function efficiently. Likewise, commercial establishments not only help concentrate their employees but to an even greater extent attract sizable numbers of customer-consumers. Many other kinds of buildings and activities, such as offices and warehouses, also attract large numbers of individuals. Congestion and confusion arise from the competition for accessible locations and the clustering of people at these favored places at particular times of the day.

Because every site in the city has a different level of accessibility to the city as a whole, places possess different locational advantages. Each location may be viewed as in competition with all others, and the land use or activity found there must possess a competitive advantage such that the activity can compete economically for that location. Highly accessible places, being most desirable, will support only those activities able to pay for the high costs these locations command. Less economically competitive activities, not able to pay the high cost of the most accessible locations, will be forced to locate in areas of secondary advantage, and so forth until the least competitive activities are relegated to the most inaccessible urban space. Very simply, this competition for urban space leads to clustering of activities and is a basic cause of traffic congestion. Activities highly competitive for accessible space include many retail establishments, certain kinds of manufacturing, offices, banks, and other businesses dependent upon accessibility. Residential land use and, especially, agriculture are significantly less competitive for central locations.

Although most of the basic causes of traffic congestion are economic, the consequences are predominantly social. No one has yet adequately determined the social cost involved in, say, a five minute traffic delay. What is the cost to society of the exhaust pollutants discharged into the air during that five minute wait? How does one measure the social disutility resulting from machine noise in the city? Finally, what is the cost of frustration to an individual delayed five minutes to breathe fumes and to hear the noise of a city creaking to a virtual halt? Although no one has been able to put a dollar tag on any of these social costs, their significance, taken up in Chapter 6, is simply enormous.

Another dimension of traffic in cities is the accident rate, an area in which the courts have attempted to translate social costs into economic ones. What is the cost of a broken leg, an amputation, a human life? Every year approximately fifty thousand people die from automobile related accidents, the equivalent of wiping off the face of the earth annually the total population of Kokomo, Indiana, or of Athens, Greece, during its Golden Age.

There are entirely different ways of looking at social costs involving what the economist would call opportunity costs. These costs comprise the potential benefits or disadvantages derived from alternative systems of transport. For example, the private automobile may be economically an efficient vehicle for intracity travel compared to the horse-drawn carriage. Which, however, has the greater social benefits? Investment in automobiles, streets, and freeways might entail potential social savings compared with other systems of urban movement, or it might mean foregoing an even greater savings possible with an alternative investment, as in some form of mass transit. The arguments among the automobile, or mass transit, or some combination of the two have not even been resolved on an economic level, let alone in terms of social benefits.

It is clear, however, that the social impact of the automobile and of mass transit is quite different. In a word, the automobile *disperses* the metropolitan area and its social space, whereas mass transit *concentrates* activities and people in urban space. As a mover of large numbers of people between a given origin and destination, mass transit cannot be even closely approached by the space-consuming automobile. The average number of passengers per automobile, including driver, is approximately 1.5, and the number of people that can be moved over an urban street is a minute fraction of the number that may be moved during the same time period by any form of mass transit, from the bus on the street to the subway. Further, because of their numbers automobiles are serious pollution contributors compared with mass transit. However, despite these relative disadvantages, the flexibility, door-to-door capability, convenience, and status value of the automobile apparently make Americans willing to devote one-fifth to one-quarter of their urban land to streets and parking for automobile use. Chapter 7 examines the issue of modes of urban travel in greater detail.

Congestion is also increasingly becoming a characteristic of communication networks, where the flow of information vital to the functioning of the city is impeded. The telephone system has a capacity limit, although it is seldom attained except during widespread emergency conditions, such as a tornado disaster, when everyone is trying to call everyone else. More commonly, communication congestion takes the subtle form of information overkill, in which the individual is assaulted with more information than he can assimilate, process, and react to. The individual becomes overstimulated, makes errors of judgment, and may become tense, irritable, and depressed. There are those who would extend these characteristics to the entire society. In the next chapter greater attention is given to problems of congestion in social communication.

Location and circulation are two sides of the same coin. When one locates his residence in the city, for example, he is at the same time determining how far he will have to travel to meet his daily living and working needs. The locations of social and economic activities depend upon transportation and communication ties. Many urban problems relate to locational maladjustments on the one hand and to circulation deficiencies on the other. Some of these deficiencies can be directly linked with major urban problems; in other cases the connections between urban problems and circulation are very indirect and subtle. This chapter has given attention to some of the more tangible difficulties of urban living relating especially to transportation. The following chapter turns to the structure and function of social communication ties as they affect the process of urbanization and its ensuing social problems.

References

1. Martin A. Knapp, "Social Effects of Transportation," *Annals of the American Academy of Political and Social Science*, Vol. 20, July - December, 1902, pp. 1 - 15, quotation, p. 3.
2. *Ibid.*, pp. 5 - 6.
3. Brian J. L. Berry, James W. Simmons, and Robert J. Tennant, "Urban Population Densities: Structure and Change," *Geographical Review*, Vol. 53, July, 1963, pp. 389 - 405.

Chapter 2

Social Interaction
and Urban Space

Many people have attempted to resolve the question of what is a city, and many answers, conditioned by the point of view of the person observing and studying the city, have been offered. The city frequently has been characterized by large population size and a high density of people per square mile. While such a definition may have been appropriate when cities constituted a tidy entity visibly distinct and separate from the agricultural landscape, cities of today have burst out of their former boundaries and have inundated the countryside to form a bewildering pattern of urban land uses. How can we tell anymore where the city begins and ends? Definitions based on legal incorporation are likewise hopelessly inadequate, as the cities have long since spilled out of their political territory. Other definitions have emphasized the "built-up" area, types of land use, which houses have one, two, or three telephones, and the extent of urban services such as water and sewage lines.

Each of these definitions, however, concentrates only on the more obvious and visible features of the urban landscape, which are merely the physical manifestation of the basic and simple desire of man to live near other men for mutual benefits. People live in cities to achieve social and economic objectives which cannot be as easily obtained in a rural or non-urban environment.

Economists and others have viewed the city as a magnet attracting rural migrants wishing to improve their economic level by living near desired employment opportunities. Many studies have been undertaken of the economic efficiency of the city in allowing ease of movement from residences to locations of economic activity. The city also creates an environment that facilitates information exchange through social communications, or social interaction. A most fundamental function of an urban area is to maximize the opportunities of contact between people and activities, activities and activities, and people and people.

Thus, the most appropriate definition of a city, in terms of the functions it actually performs, involves transportation and communication. One may usefully conceptualize a metropolis by the nature, intensity, and extent of social communications that take place. Since the opportunities for social contact and information exchange are distributed differently within the city, transportation and communication may be viewed as key processes in the operation of the urban system. The tremendous variety of opportunities for social contact within the city have given rise to a social structure that sets the urban area apart from the rapidly contracting traditional agrarian social system. It is this social structure of the city, here viewed geographically, that constitutes an essential element of what a city is.

One may contrast the huge engine of communication that is the metropolis with the social ties within the small agrarian community of the past. In the latter the chance that any one individual would have contact with any other individual was fairly high. Even a new member of the community could make contact with virtually all other individuals in a very short time. Everyone knew what everyone else was doing. The amount of information to be exchanged was more in balance with the potentialities of the communication system, and potential contacts did not greatly exceed actual contacts. The social relations in the agrarian society were highly biased toward members of the extended family, and the intensity of social interaction was greatest with relatives.

As a city increases in size, the potential for contact among individuals increases geometrically. When the city is small and the number of potential contacts is not far above the actual contacts, fairly complete information exchange is possible. As the social system enlarges with city growth, the gap increases between potential and actual social contacts. The communication system becomes biased or differentiated along selected lines to form particular communication networks, representing an individual's social contacts. When information exchange becomes divided among defined channels or networks, no one has full knowledge of the total pool of information. Since the actual number of contacts per unit of time for an individual will reach a threshold, owing to constraints of time and energy, the width of the gap between total and actual information grows primarily as a function of the expansion of potential contacts.

Here we note an ironic situation with respect to social communication in the city. Each individual theoretically has potential access

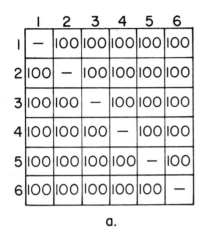
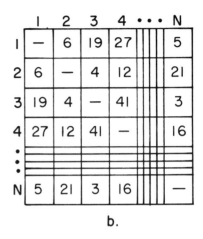

a.   **b.**

Figure 2.1: The rows represent individuals originating information and the columns show information received by individuals. In Figure 2.1a there is a free flow of information as each receiver obtains 100 percent of all the information sent out. However, in Figure 2.1b there are various barriers to the easy flow of information and individuals receive only a portion of the total information originated.

to the city's enormous information pool. Yet as the pool grows with the size of the city, the fraction of that pool known to the average individual shrinks! No doubt the very largest cities reach thresholds of diminishing communication returns.

Figure 2.1 illustrates the situation described above. The rows of the table represent persons originating information and the columns show those who receive the information. (The diagonal elements are omitted, since these would depict an individual communicating with himself!) In Figure 2.1a, each receiver obtains 100 percent of the information originating from each person. Here, we have the case in which everyone knows everyone else's business, a condition possible in only a very small social group lacking barriers to communication. This may be contrasted with Figure 2.1b in which the number of persons is large and the amount of information received by any one person from any other person is generally small. This figure is symmetric, which means that we are assuming a two-way flow of information among the people. (In many real-world situations, the flow of information may be stronger in one direction than the other.) Figure 2.1b is more characteristic of the metropolis than is the "free information flow" example. It suggests that social connections in the city are frequent, diffused among a large number of individuals, and biased or organized around particular networks through which information moves.

Although the city has been described above as a mechanism for facilitating information exchange through social communication, it is an imperfect mechanism when compared to the complete information flow example. Three principal limitations to social communication exist in the modern city. The first is the inescapable and oppressive burden of space itself. Urban space imposes barriers between all its residents, but these are unequal barriers. The transportation route system itself is confined to specific portions of the city and creates barriers to movement although it is intended to enhance interaction among the population. Routes simply do not permit equal speed and ease of movement in all directions. Some routes are always slow, congested, and roundabout. The expense, effort, and time spent crossing urban space must always be weighed against the anticipated advantages to be gained at the end of the trip. Many of the basic problems of the city as a social environment, examined more fully below, can be traced to an inequality among its residents in their ability to overcome urban space.

A second restraint on urban social interaction is social status, especially as manifested among the social neighborhoods of urban areas. Numerous studies have documented that social connections are more likely among those of similar socioeconomic status than among those of quite different social status. Because of the tendency toward residential clustering, neighborhood barriers are created, maintained, and intensified by intervening distance. The chance that a resident from a high-income neighborhood will have social contact with an individual living in a low-income area is even less than the distance between such households would suggest. Urban space is rendered unequal by the diversity of human activities.

A third restraint on the easy flow of information is the problem of congestion and overload. Traffic congestion limits the physical mobility of a traveler just as too much information in too brief a period of time overburdens the mind. Whereas those in the small agrarian settlement long for gossip, the metropolitan dweller seeks privacy as protection from the near infinity of contacts from which he may choose. Likewise he may retreat into simplistic explanations, embrace stereotypes, or latch onto insignificant detail because of the huge volume of information with which the urban dweller is almost constantly assaulted. Overloads on the social communication system, resulting from the inherent advantages of urbanism, lead to the virtual paralysis of the urban system's greatest asset, information access. The broader the range of choices from which one must choose, the greater will be the chance that the best choice will not be made, and the greater is the apprehension that the wrong choice in fact is being made. One reacts to too much information stimulus by ignoring large parts of it, and an essential function of the city becomes obscured.

Many powerful social forces and institutions have been created to maintain a cohesive and functional urban environment for social communication. Fundamental among these is the complementarity of social roles. Of necessity a tremendous range of roles has been created within the city. A single individual may play several roles in different social settings. This role-playing sets up situations in which social communication may take place along reasonably comfortable lines for reasonably defined purposes. Much of this role-playing in fact is conditioned by the need for a division of labor in information exchange; social roles are a form of societal organization within which information moves.

Although the family, which values the freedom to pursue interpersonal contacts selectively, is still the basic social unit, other formalized organizations have been created to facilitate the operation of urban society. These institutions are administered largely through a hierarchy of interpersonal contact in which information exchange is critical to successful functioning. The spatial concentration of these organizations within cities imposes a spatial clustering of interpersonal ties in which the participants normally have relatively little choice in selecting each other. Furthermore, these organizations have taken a dominant position in society relative to the family. The net result is a pattern of interpersonal relations in which professional or job contacts have come in part to replace emotional and intimate social ties. However, the large quantity of transitory and perfunctory contacts assists the selection process for developing closer social relations within cities.

One answer to the question of what characterizes a city, then, is its performance in making possible a myriad of choices of social communication and information exchange. "It is the multiplicity of different facilities and of persons, and the wide choice of potential quick contacts among them, that makes the metropolis what it is."[1] The barriers of distance and socioeconomic status limit the flow of social communication, as does the problem of congestion and communication overload. Information tends to flow along fairly repetitious channels (as encouraged or discouraged by distance, status, and congestion) to form definable communication networks. These networks may be solidified, modified, and extended both by family preferences for social selection and by institutional organization. Maintenance of networks for information access may be enhanced by the varying social roles that individuals play in the city.

The Neighborhood As a Social Environment

Often we tend to view the city as a mosaic of residential neighborhoods. The ethnic residential concentrations, especially those of the past, call our attention to distinct neighborhood units. But the term neighborhood has also come to mean a great many other things. Nearly every urban resident views himself as living in a neighborhood, and if asked he would have at least a vague notion of the extent and composition of "his neighborhood." He would normally perceive it as a good place to live, where the tempo of living is comfortable, where a routine of events can be expected, and most of all where a psychological sense of belonging is maintained.

The planner views the neighborhood more objectively. He sees it as an organized community of people and buildings, a layout of streets and services, an area of socioeconomic homogenity. The planner colors his maps of neighborhoods with different shades, depending on the quality and quantity of housing, age of population, income level, and educational achievement. The neighborhood is seen as a planning unit, though rarely a planned unit.

Others view the neighborhood from their own peculiar vantage points. The geographer emphasizes an analysis of the similarities and differences from place to place within the neighborhood and the connections between places. The sociologist may focus on the socioeconomic structure of the resident population. The economist will see its economic function in terms of purchasing power, consumption preferences, or tax base. The voting history and political attitudes become of interest to the political scientist in understanding neighborhoods. Clearly, no single definition or concept of the neighborhood is everywhere accepted.

One prominent thread, however, runs across each of these different ways of looking at the neighborhood. The glue, to mix a metaphor, which somehow binds the neighborhood together is social cohesion, as manifested through the interlinking networks of social communications. Viewed in this sense, a neighborhood consists of individuals who interact with one another or identify with one another through actual or imagined ties. This identification may simply be the result of social status or ethnic characteristics. More commonly, true neighborhoods exist because of the interlocking pattern of communication, acquaintanceship, and friendship fostered by residential proximity.

Several very interesting studies have been carried out on the process of marriage mate selection within cities.[2] These studies have invariably found that distance or residential separation plays a significant role in the selection process. Two interrelated factors are involved. First is the fact that mate selection most frequently occurs within the same or similar socioeconomic levels. Because of the residential clustering of like status groups, it follows that there is a greater chance of mate selections from nearby residential neighborhoods. The second factor is the normal distance drop-off in contacts and in social communication away from the residential location. This factor operates through geographically bound

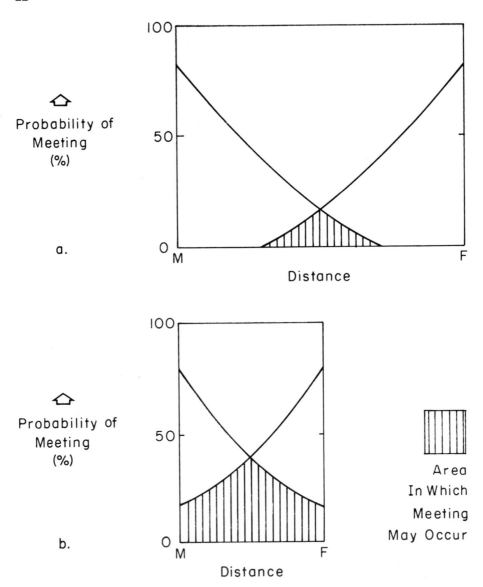

Figure 2.2: The probability that any two individuals will meet depends on their residential distance apart. In Figure 2.2a there is only a small chance of contact because of the great distances involved; however, in Figure 2.2b the possibilities of contact are fairly high, as shown by the shaded area indicating probability of meeting.

public school districts and locally focused organizations, including clubs and churches.

The probability that any two individuals will meet is in part conditioned by the space separating them. Additionally, space may impose a barrier to the courtship by reducing the frequency of contact where great distances are involved. Figure 2.2a demonstrates a hypothetical meeting situation for two individuals, M and F, who are separated by a relatively long distance. Assuming a given decline with distance in the probability of meeting for each person, one can see that the chance is rather small of contact between these two people. In contrast, Figure 2.2b shows individuals M and F located closer together, with the same decay over distance in the probability of meeting. Here, however, the likelihood of contact is greatly enhanced by the small distance. As noted earlier, the chance that one individual will meet another declines away from his household, as his typical living and acting space normally envelops his residence owing to the time, cost, and effort necessary to move through urban space.

Marriage normally requires a period of courtship interaction. To say it scientifically, a sufficiently high level of anticipated utility or satisfaction must be associated with overcoming the barrier of distance for the courtship to continue, though many other barriers may cause it to fizzle as well. The higher the amount of potential courtship interaction, it has been found, the greater the likelihood of marriage.

Every marriageable individual may be considered a "selector." Every selector has a geographically restricted area at a given point in time in which to carry out the "search" for an "eligible." The selector is also part of a spatially restricted group of eligibles. Contact among eligibles is a function of social status, mobility, distance, and to some extent age. Contact may be facilitated by "organizational points," such as churches or taverns which function in part to augment potential contacts. An inevitable, and important, function of colleges and universities is to bring many eligibles into close spatial proximity, forming dormitory or university neighborhoods.

In fact, several studies of the social relations of individuals have been made of campus married housing units, dormitories, offices, and even classrooms.[3] These findings reveal that relatively short distances are significant in establishing social contacts and friendship patterns. The architectural and geographical arrangement of housing units inevitably acts to bring certain families and individuals into greater than average contact. Since an important ingredient in friendship formation is frequency of contact and communication — everything else being equal — the arrangement of the housing environment is a substantial force both in acquaintanceship and friendship formation. The same goes for the classroom. Seating patterns lead to acquaintanceship, enhancing the opportunity for friendship formation.

Although the spatial arrangement of a neighborhood or a room may affect the frequency of communication among individuals, psychological factors help determine the quality and intensity of the relationship. It is especially during the early stages of acquaintanceship development that distance exerts its strongest effect. Personality attraction, ego completion, complementary needs, and compatibility form the psychological basis of friendship, and these qualities may overcome adverse geographical conditions. The classic case, of course, of overcoming geographical distance is the marriage decision, in which the residential distance between individuals becomes considerably reduced.

Not only may marital mate selection be influenced by the neighborhood but so too are political opinions and attitudes. Political scientists have long noticed the fact that political values vary geographically from one part of the city to another. Some neighborhoods are predictably conservative, some liberal; pollsters know certain areas will vote Republican, others Democratic. One obvious explanation for shared neighborhood opinion is that such communities, as we have already seen, tend to be homogeneous in population composition. It is not surprising that those of similar socioeconomic background and demographic makeup will share like political feelings.

A second fundamental influence upon local political opinion is the social communication network, through which selective political information flows. Attitudes are partly the product of past accumulations of information. The numerous personal contacts within the neighborhood, particularly as they may occur at community functions and organizations, tend to support commonly held political feelings and to ignore or suppress deviant views. The neighborhood, by placing many individuals of similar status near one another, helps establish, maintain, and reinforce particular political values.

The essential characteristic defining "neighborhood" is the degree of interaction and the amount of information exchanged among the different people included within the neighborhood. The key element is information flow, as it is through these transactions that a sense of community may emerge. Commonly shared knowledge, and hence attitudes, become geographically anchored in particular areas of the city, mediated through interlocking social communication networks. Members of a neighborhood having a mutually shared information base are most likely to behave in similar ways, whether in consumption patterns or at the ballot box. Since the amount of shared information normally declines with distance, so too can one expect common behavioral traits to become less frequent away from the heart of a neighborhood, whether in manner of speech or in preference for a particular shopping facility.

Up to this point, we have accepted the assumption that the

neighborhood constitutes a geographically bounded and contiguous area. This assumption is somewhat improper, even though it does not invalidate what we have said before. The basic difficulty with our assumption has been that it fails to take sufficiently into account automobile mobility and the impact it has had on the traditional neighborhood concept.

The neighborhood still exists, as long as we define it, as we have, by an interlinking of communication channels. Even the automobile has not been able to destroy totally the old-fashioned barrier of distance for interpersonal information exchange, although the telephone has proven a handy substitute for many, but not all, occasions. The neighborhood in the modern city has become much more geographically diffused and fragmented, even though it continues to hang together functionally and to serve the social needs of the people perhaps better than in the past. Just as the automobile has extended one's geographic choice of where to live and work, it also has fostered greater selectivity in friendship development by providing a wider range of choice among potential contacts.

Today, proportionately fewer friends are likely to reside in close spatial proximity to one's residence than was typical in the past. Also, friendship formation is less likely to be locally based and more characteristically established at outside activities such as work, which is itself less spatially tied to home locations than in the past. It is not uncommon to hear reports of apartment dwellers, for example, who have lived for years without becoming acquainted with any of their apartment dwelling neighbors. The neighborhood of such people most definitely is diffused away from the brick, board, and mortar neighborhood concept of the urban past.

The new concept of neighborhood has meant a readjustment of social organization. Many people moving into a city may conclude that the city is unfriendly and cold because the physical neighborhood in which they live does not satisfy their social needs. Community identification does not emerge, and an essential element in man's territoriality is unfulfilled. Thus a constraint to releasing man's social energy is placed on an avowedly social animal, as the mechanism for socialization in the modern city is unlike the locally based social system in the agrarian community of the past. Now vast gulfs of nonpersons exist between islands of friends, and the information exchange, integral to the sense of neighborhood, must overcome the barriers of city streets and communication congestion to survive. The thread running through the neighborhood of the past, which we have identified as information exchange, is now stretched and woven far and wide in the immense fabric of the city. We therefore turn to a consideration of the individual and his social communications.

Social Interaction and the Individual

In looking at social interaction from the point of view of the individual it is appropriate to focus upon the actual network of social linkages which the individual has with his various social contacts. We have earlier considered the large potential urban space in which social contact may occur. For convenience, we will term this *opportunity space*.[4] Figure 2.3 depicts the hypothetical opportunity space of one individual; this space is coextensive with the urban area. It is from this enormous pool of possibilities that social contacts are made and social communications take place. Most of these opportunities remain unknown to an individual.

As a subset of opportunity space, every individual has an *action space* which comprises the group of acquaintances and past contacts. Action space is simply that part of opportunity space about which an individual has information. While opportunity space reflects objective reality, action space represents a perception of reality which follows the past experiences, characteristics, and preferences of the individual. Thus the opportunity space is the same for every inhabitant of the urban area; the action space, however, is different for every individual.

Two features of action space deserve our attention. The first is its geographical extent within the city, anchored on an individual's residential location. Although information about social acquaintances is dispersed over a wide portion of the urban area, a considerable local bias is likely to prevail, reflected in a clustered arrangement of possible social ties. Since one's normal living space is centered on the home location, more information will normally be available about the local area.

The second attribute of action space we may call *utility*, or the level of satisfaction anticipated from a social contact. The direct measurement of this satisfaction or psychological utility to be derived from a social tie is very difficult, but it is clear that some set of factors is consciously or unconsciously considered. The selection of a certain individual as a social contact at a given time indicates an expected level of comfort above that anticipated from any other possible social tie. Each acquaintance within one's action space is subjectively assigned a weight depending on the level of expected psychological utility. One factor against which this utility must be balanced is that of travel effort (time, distance, and cost). It is easier to maintain a close friendship with a person living next door, all things being equal, than with someone across town, and easier to visit frequently someone across town than a person out-of-state. Thus action space has two related components: a geographical extent and a net psychological utility subjectively assigned at any point in time to a possible social tie within the socially bounded urban space.

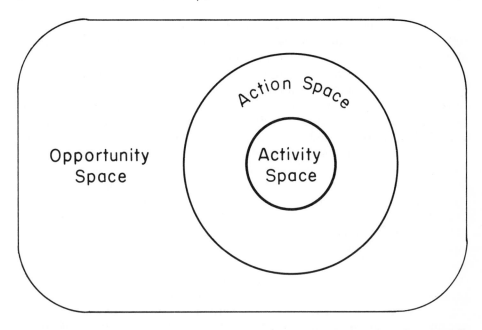

Figure 2.3: Hypothetical spaces for an individual. Activity space refers to the area of the city frequented in one's day-to-day movements; action space is that area of the city which one knows about, at least in some vague way; opportunity space represents the objective reality of city areas. The knowledge one has of the spatial locations in a city determines the extent of his activity and action space.

Finally Figure 2.3 suggests that within the realm of available information about social acquaintances (action space) there exists for an individual a smaller space which represents the normally utilized set of social ties. The latter is *activity space*, again focused on the residential location. Connecting this activity space to an individual is his own unique social communications network through which he disseminates and receives information. Geographically, activity space has an extent and intensity of use, variable over periods of time as well as among different people.

The activity space of any person or household stems from characteristics of lifestyle. Socioeconomic and demographic qualities mold the life patterns of households; combinations of status and stage in family life cycle influence residential location, leisure time availability, and patterns of consumption. All of these factors lead to differing opportunities and preferences for social contact. Some families or individuals may have a significantly larger action space in which to carry out their lifestyle. One person during his social leisure may drink in a bar, another may watch television with the family, a third may attend a church service, and a fourth may visit a friend. These activities, in addition to reflecting lifestyle differences, bring about varying opportunities for altering the existing activity space as new information becomes available.

In addition to these characteristics internal to households, two types of external factors are important determinants of one's social activity space. When the spatial distribution of social acquaintanceship is thinly spread, as in a rural area, activity space may be more extensive than in a more densely populated urban area. Closely related to the internal factors are the connections within the social communication network itself. An individual linked with many organizational points has access to a larger total population than does one whose social network is of simple functional and geographic structure. Again, the larger the action space, the greater the activity space is likely to be. Thus the two main external determinants of activity space are the distribution of social ties and the structure of the social communication network.

The social ties of any individual may be graphically expressed by the spatial arrangement of his social communications network in which geographic structure represents functional characteristics. Figure 2.4 shows a variety of contrasting social networks for some hypothetical individual, I. In Figure 2.4a, the network has a simple structure, only three friendship connections, each friend located near the residence of I. Furthermore, there is no friendship connection among any of I's three friends. A slightly more complex example is given in Figure 2.4b, in which the dashed lines show friendship among all of I's five friends. These two examples illustrate the contrast between an unconnected and a connected social communications network, the latter carrying more redundant information and being more closely knit.

Many people are members of some group, club, or organization, either voluntarily (as a church) or through work affiliation, for example. Figure 2.4c displays a social communications network with both localized and dispersed elements, as well as ties generated through organizational points (workplace and church). We assume that colleagues at work and friendships through church are each fully connected by friendship ties. A hierarchial communications network is described in Figure 2.4d, in which a particular organizational point is connected to a second through a friendship tie, and so on. Such a network best illustrates a complex of business or political connections. Except for the hierarchial arrangement, this network is similar to that in Figure 2.4c.

The rapidity of change within the social communications system gives insights into some of the most interesting features of urban socializing, as social ties are highly variable over time. It is here useful to look at social ties in terms of urban travel undertaken for the purpose of visiting and expending social leisure with friends, neighbors, and relatives. In ad-

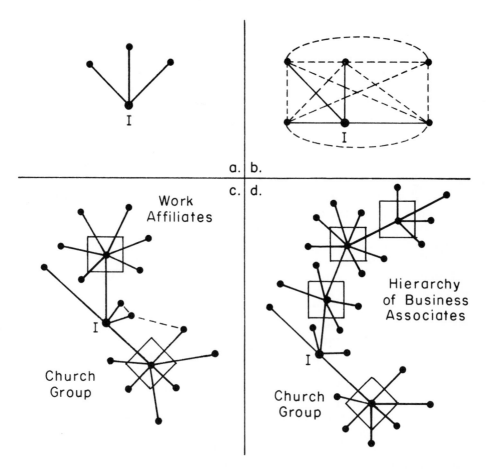

Figure 2.4: Hypothetical social communications networks of four individuals, a, b, c, and d. Solid lines show friendship connections between the individual, I, and his friends; dashed lines show friendship among I's friends (connected network). Clusters of friendships may occur at work, business, or church locations, for example.

dition to actual travel over urban space for socializing purposes, the pattern of telephone connections also depicts the social communications network, both telephone and travel probably resulting in similar social patterns over a long period of time. Social travel is one process by which socializing may take place when the parties are spatially separated from one another. Over a sufficiently long time, one's social travel has enough repetitive characteristics in order to speak of it, as we have been, as forming an activity space held together by a social communications network. Normally, there are significant temporal changes in one's social trip-making.

First of all, social travel varies by time of day, with the bulk of social trips during weekdays occurring during the late afternoon and evening. There is also a tendency for social trips to take place over the noon lunch hour. These trips reflect the working population, and many social visits among those not in the labor force (housewives and students) are spread throughout the morning and afternoon hours. Weekends, however, have a quite different pattern of social trips, and a large proportion of all social trips occur on weekends. During weekends, travel to visit is most often concentrated in the afternoon and evening, there being little discernible bunching of these trips over the noon hour. Social travel also depends on the time of year. In areas of cold winter climates, with shorter daylight hours, there seems to be less visiting and outdoor socializing than during the summer months. Holidays exert a well-known influence on social travel, with peaking over the Christmas - New Year, Easter, and Thanksgiving holidays. Summer vacation periods, moreover, affect the frequency and characteristics of social trips. The peaks in automobile fatalities at predictable times of the year are largely related to social travel.

The way in which friendships are formed sheds some light on a different aspect of social dynamics. Friendship may develop from neighborhood interaction, from contact with school chums of the past, from membership in formal and informal clubs and social organizations, through work affiliations, through travel, and through other friendships. In each of these cases, with the probable exception of travel, the geographical locations of the friends may be either local or city-wide. Whereas neighborhood interaction normally results in a short-distance social trip, friendships formed within a neighborhood may later mean a long-distance trip if the friend or oneself has changed residence. Likewise a school buddy may continue to live nearby because he attended a local high school, for example, or farther away in the city if residential change has occurred. Friendship formations through both clubs and work may generate either short of long social trips, with some predominance of the latter likely. Many friendships are made through another friend or even through one's children (especially at the neighborhood level).

As we have previously noted, the lifestyle of an individual affects the structure of his social communications network. It also influences the process of friendship formation. An atheist will not likely form his set of friends through a church group, nor will an unemployed laborer be able to make friends through work. The process of friendship development typical of a particular lifestyle in turn has an effect on one's social communications network over time. It is a two-way cause and effect. In particular, the opportunities for new friendship formation, a function of the existing network of social ties and the lifestyle of the individual, affects the dynamic changes in the structure of the social network.

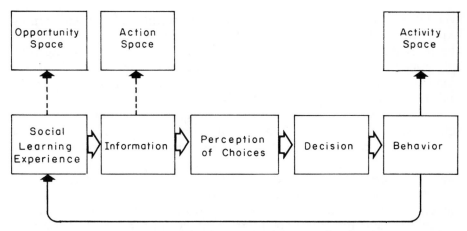

Figure 2.5: The process of friendship formation when one is faced with a new social environment. Note the importance of learning and information on opportunity, action, and activity space.

Furthermore, friendship patterns change over time with changes in lifestyle, especially as brought about by shifts in socioeconomic status and family structure. The old story that with upward social mobility one gives up his long-time friends to seek new and different social relations is often all too true, though perhaps we should say merely that an adjustment takes place in the social communications network. Increased socioeconomic status may permit a residential shift into another neighborhood in which a different set of social ties is possible. A promotion may mean association with a different group of colleagues. A growing family may necessitate a residential change to more spacious quarters, or a wife's going back to work after raising the family may provide new social contacts.

What happens to one's socialization when one is placed in an unfamiliar geographical setting, say as the result of moving into a new city? This question is a common one because of the large number of migrants to cities, from both rural to urban movement and the now more common inter-urban migration. Although the specific answer to this question will be different for each case, certain features will operate in general for all individuals. We will assume the new migrant has no friendship ties in the urban area to which he has moved, though many migrants in fact will choose a destination because of information about the new community passed on by a social contact, often a relative. How will the social network develop?

Reference to Figure 2.5 suggests the several steps encountered in the process of friendship formation and the development of the social communications network. Social learning will begin almost immediately when one is placed into an unfamiliar urban setting. The initial learning experience will be especially dependent on the lifestyle characteristics of the individual or family. Social learning will provide an opening peep into a small component of the overall opportunity space. This learning process is translated into information regarding the opportunity space, and a limited action space becomes formed.

The next step is based on the subjective perception of the social opportunities which are known. A ranking of some sort is given to these known social sources. One will seldom rank in order each possible social tie from first to last, but will group his choices into roughly three categories: unsatisfactory, satisfactory, and optimal. The latter will be reserved for only the most intimate social contacts. In the very early stages, the three categories may have an unequal balance, as a majority of possible social contacts may be lumped into a single group. It is common for the unsatisfactory category to be perceived as no category at all, as those falling into this group are simply not considered as possible social contacts or future friends.

As a consequence of the perception of the social action space, certain decisions will be consciously or subconsciously arrived at for accepting or initiating social contact. These decisions are manifested in social behavior, such as a telephone conversation or a social trip. Social behavior allows the opportunity for further social learning, which provides a basis for additional knowledge to color perceptions, in turn giving a foundation for future decisions and subsequent behavior. As learning accumulates and thus widens the range of the action space, changes may occur in the earlier ranking of choices. Getting to know someone better may raise the initial estimate, or it may lower it. The infusion of other social acquaintances may cause a fundamental re-evaluation of the previous alternatives.

In any case, what ensues is an extension and modification of the social communications network and its geographical manifestation, activity space. While during the early stages of acquaintanceship exploration the network enlarges rapidly and may undergo several modifications, a quiescent period is eventually encountered in which a type of social equilibrium is achieved. In this stage, there is a balance between the quality and quantity of social need and the options for its satisfactory expression. Habitual social behavior then becomes common. This quiescent state may be temporarily upset by a sudden change in socioeconomic status or in family structure. Old age often brings retractions in the network, and social isolation.

Concluding Remarks

Communication networks are a fundamental component in the organization of urban life. The urban network as a whole is an invisible structure of connections through which flows information that permits the city to function, change, and grow. Linking the geographically separated parts of the city are the urban arteries, veins, vessels, and capillaries that maintain a living and dynamic city. The structure of connections, though not expressed on the urban landscape in the physical manner of streets and highways, nevertheless constitutes the mechanism leading to man's behavior. The network is the structure, the information the process, and behavior the manifestation. Out of the behavior of urban man follows urban change.

Since communication networks provide the organizational basis for urban life, their effects are found in the geographical arrangements of people and activities in the city. When distance was a powerful barrier in the past, networks were more locally articulated, and physical structures more easily identified and coextensive with social cohesion. A new concept in social cohesion is now imposed on the city with the areal stretching and functional complexity of communication networks. The most difficult problems of adjustment in the urban environment involve coping with the social communication network. The many frustrations of city life stem from the changes in this social network, the same changes which propel the city's growth and efficiency.

Perhaps some day we will more easily be able to adjust the changes within the urban system to the social needs of the individual. It is far too common now for a beneficial change in the city to work to the detriment of certain groups and individuals. In Chapter 4 we will return to this issue, examining the black city within the city and how the social changes in these two cities have pulled toward opposite ends.

References

1. Karl W. Deutsch, "On Social Communications and the Metropolis," *Daedalus*, Vol. 90, Winter 1961, pp. 99 - 110.

2. A.M. Katz and R. Hill, "Residential Propinquity and Marital Selection: A Review of Theory, Method, and Fact," *Marriage and Family Living*, Vol. 20, 1958, pp. 27 - 35 and N. R. Ramsøy, "Assortative Mating and the Structure of Cities," *American Sociological Review*, Vol. 31, 1966, pp. 773 - 786.

3. L. Festinger, *et al.*, *Social Pressures in Informal Groups*, New York: Harpers, 1950; R. F. Priest and J. Sawyer, "Proximity and Peership: Bases of Balance in Interpersonal Attraction," *American Journal of Sociology*, Vol. 72, 1967, pp. 633 - 649.

4. Frank E. Horton and David R. Reynolds, "Effects of Urban Spatial Structure on Individual Behavior," *Economic Geography*, Vol. 47, 1971, pp. 36 - 48.

Chapter 3

Social Status and
the Journey to Work

In every urban area of any size, there is a striking tendency for people to live near people who are like themselves. This preference, though varying from person to person, is sufficiently strong that residential neighborhoods identified by social status can be found in every city. Furthermore, the type of location is quite similar from one large city to the next; the black ghetto, for example, is typically located downtown near the business district, whereas those of high status typically live in selected suburban neighborhoods. The urban area may be viewed as a complex of social areas, in part overlapping with one another, but basically distinct units of social space.

In this chapter we will consider the varying composition of residential social space, the changing employment location in the city, and the adjusting pattern of the journey to work for different socioeconomic groups. Not only does the city bring people and activities into potential contact through proximity and the technology of overcoming physical space, but the city also offers a wide scope of opportunities for changing residential location as well as workplace location. In addition to the observable daily ebb and flow of traffic there is the traffic in households shifting residential addresses. Even though many residential locations exist, not all households perceive them as equally satisfactory, desirable, or attainable. Common preferences lead to common behavior in residential selection. At the same time that residential mobility occurs, employment continues to undergo locational shifts, bringing about inevitable changes in traffic patterns and congestion. The current socio-geographic space of the city represents a dynamic process of adjustment induced by myriad factors. Let us consider what this space looks like.

Residential location and social status

There are four essential family characteristics that combine to influence the residential location decision and consequently the social living space within the city. The first is income. The price of housing varies within the urban area, as we have seen in Chapter I, and it is apparent that low-income households cannot afford the highest housing prices. All income groups, except the very highest, are thus constrained to some degree in residential choice. A second and closely related factor is social status. A primary determinant of status is income itself, although one may attain high status by activities only indirectly related to income. One may wish to live in a particular neighborhood for reasons of status, and different families will place different values on neighborhood prestige.

A third characteristic influencing residential location, and one operating more or less independently of the first two, is family structure. A family typically goes through several stages in its life cycle. First the family consists of man and wife. This initial stage is usually followed by the addition of children. The family attains its maximum size; the children grow up, and eventually leave home. The family's size declines, the age of the individuals increases until one or both die. At each stage in the cycle, preferences for residential location change and intra-urban migration frequently occurs. Thus family structure affects the type of home preferred, which also varies with location in the city.

The final factor relating to residential choice is mobility preference, translated directly into location. Families with high mobility preferences are free to select a residence at a greater distance from work, shopping, and other activities. Families placing a premium on little daily urban travel choose a residence near desired activity points. Mobility is related both to income and social status, as well as to stage in family cycle. It is well known that high-income and high status families are more mobile. Older, small families are among the least mobile, whereas younger, large families are often the most mobile, especially when there are several individuals of driving age and socioeconomic status is high.

Figure 3.1a shows the residential structure of the city of Chicago classified by social space and family structure; 3.1b describes the salient characteristics of the areas. The desire of many is to move upward on the scale of social space, at the same time as they inexorably slide to the left, pushed along by time. The black ghetto in general occupies a part of the lower right quadrant of Figure 3.1b, having large families with a low average age. Sharing this quadrant are also the poor white families, perhaps living in public housing, in the early to middle stages of family

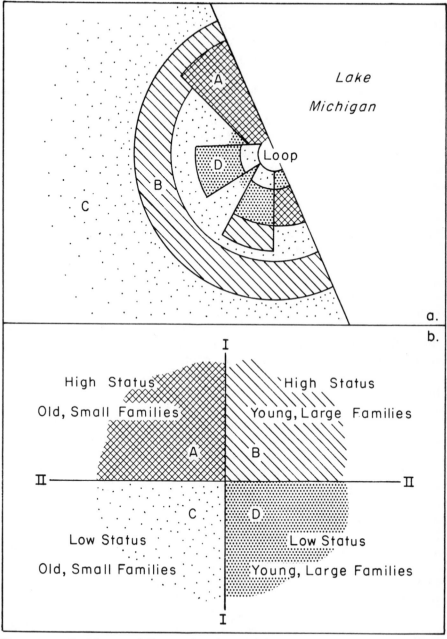

Figure 3.1: Social areas of Chicago, based on two factors, socioeconomic status (I) and stage in family cycle (II). Definite residential areas emerge by combining these two factors. Taken from Brian J. L. Berry and Frank E. Horton, *Geographic Perspectives on Urban Systems: With Integrated Readings* (Englewood Cliffs, N.J.: Prentice-Hall, 1970) Figure 10-31, p. 379 (based on Philip H. Rees, *The Factorial Ecology of Metropolitan Chicago*, M.A. thesis, University of Chicago, 1968).

formation. The lower left quadrant similarly represents low status groups, but in the later stages of the family cycle. The lower two quadrants include the blue collar workers, ranging from craftsmen and foremen at the top of blue collar scale to unskilled laborers.

The upper two quadrants depict the higher status groups. On the right-hand side are the new suburban areas consisting of newly formed, large, and growing families. At the upper left are the longer-established high status areas, with relatively few children, and older average age. Such areas are typically found both within the political city itself, as well as in selected older suburbs. Colleges and university dormitories might be represented at the extreme upper right of the scale, whereas "skid row" would be at the extreme lower left.

We ought to trace the development of urban social space through several shifts and stages over time. The geography of residential social status is best treated with reference to transportation technology, here following a useful synopsis discussed by Ornati in a recently published book entitled *Transportation Needs of the Poor.* Five stages are presented, diagramed in Figure 3.2.

In the initial stage the city was young and small; the central business district, with manufacturing scattered in and around, dominated the city's economic structure. Muscle-power supplied the transportation. The rich, as even today in cities of the developing world, tended to occupy the more accessible core. Because differences in accessibility in the small city were not large, the poor were often scattered helter-skelter throughout the city, although with greater concentrations at the less accessible edges.

The second stage was initiated by the development of streetcars and commuter railroads. The rich continued to reside near the city core, but the middle-income group began migrating outward to more distant locations now made accessible. The very rich felt no need to change residence, the investment in the substantial homes of the city core maintaining their traditional status. However, the out-migration of the middle-income families brought the rich and poor into close contact, and the physical distance between the two groups was now markedly at variance with their social distance. A residential disequilibrium had been created, as social preferences for individual contact and status considerations were placed in conflict through the geography of residential social status.

The next stage was characterized by out-migration of a sizable proportion of the upper-income group to create a suburban ring around the city. The city consisted of both middle and low status groups, the latter more concentrated near the core of urban areas. A few of the rich continued to reside in the core, mainly the older, smaller high status families. High-income families at an earlier stage of the life cycle were more likely to live in the surburban ring. The principal transportation ad-

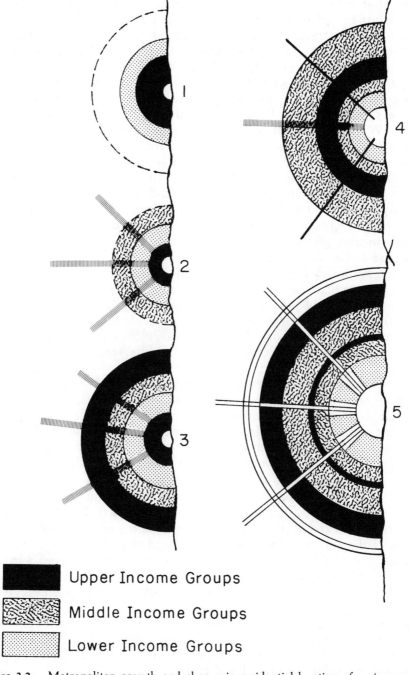

Figure 3.2: Metropolitan growth and change in residential location of socioeconomic groups in a hypothetical urban area. Taken from Oscar A. Ornati, *Transportation Needs of the Poor: A Case Study of New York City* (New York: Preager, 1969) pp. 8 - 9.

vance that induced the high-income families to migrate was automobile ownership, in this early stage only affordable by the relatively well-to-do. Although the streetcar and the commuter railroad helped create the scattered isolated suburbs, the automobile filled in the surburban ring with nearly continuous residential land use. The automobile ownership of the rich allowed a social equilibrium to be established, save in the very core where the poor encroached upon the rich on the one hand and where business expanded into the older wealthy area on the other.

With widespread automobile usage, the middle-income group now was able to generate stage four, in which many families in this income spread took up suburban living. A second suburban ring came to encircle the city. Most traffic focused on the city's business district, to which access was easy in contrast to multi-directional movement within the city itself. The families filling up the second suburban ring tended to be at early stages in the family cycle, the major difference between the middle-income group in the city and that in the suburb being family structure rather than social status.

Continued improvements in the automobile and in highway facilities have produced a fifth and current stage in which upper-income families have established a third suburban ring at a substantial distance from the city's business core. Although a sizable proportion of the labor force of the third ring works in the city core, more and more find employment in suburban locations. It is the middle status households that dominate the first suburban ring, along with high status families in the later part of the family life cycle. A growing portion of the city consists of the poor, constrained by housing costs to the oldest and most densely populated areas. Wherever transportation arteries make it possible and low cost housing is available, the poor move out to a few nearby suburban residential areas, forced by urban renewal or induced by workplace suburbanization. In such locations, automobile ownership is mandatory.

These five stages did not evolve in any city in exactly the way described in the idealized example. There were as many variations as cities; yet the same basic pattern was repeated in each. The most common departure from the idealized evolutionary scheme was the discontinuous nature of the various suburban rings. Instead of the third ring, for example, being a continuous belt encircling the city, it in fact appears in most cities as fragmented and confined to one or more sectors located at the urban periphery. Likewise, the second suburban ring is nearly everywhere fragmented, and the first ring in no city displays the neat geometric arrangement suggested by the foregoing illustration. The same conditions are true with respect to the low-income families. There is a marked tendency toward their residential concentration in the city center, but there are exceptions in individual cities.

The Moving Job Market

Compared to residences, the location of jobs in the city has generally been slower to change, and patterns of workplaces are likely to be more variable from city to city. The job shifts that have occurred, however, have followed the basic principle of decentralization, i.e., the outward expansion of jobs away from the city core into suburban locations. The rate of decentralization has varied widely for different occupations; now there are rather considerable contrasts in workplace patterns among the occupational groups.

In the early era of city growth and development, there was a definite concentration of jobs in the city core. It was here that the railroads usually terminated or cut through the city and loaded and unloaded cargo. A central location for handling was ideal because it held the highest level of accessibility to all parts of the small but growing city. Furthermore, retailing and service activities located at the core for reasons of maximum accessibility to consumers. The existence of several kinds of retail and service activities in close proximity meant that comparison shopping could occur and that various activities could be visited on a single trip. The railroad, which provided most small settlements with delivery of retail goods, found its centrally located terminal facilities ideally suited to serve the growing manufacturing activities springing up in many parts of the country. Being primarily dependent on rail service for assembling materials and distributing finished products, most early manufacturing plants recognized the area near the city's core as an ideal site. Access to the labor market was at the same time maximized.

As the city expanded outward residentially, the growth in retailing and industrial jobs became more and more concentrated in and near the central core. Institutional jobs, such as those in government, education, and hospitals, also tended to develop at the city core. A definite land use arrangement came to characterize city after city, with the core devoted to government, retail, and service activities. The area surrounding the core consisted of wholesaling and manufacturing establishments, often found in one or two sectors adjacent to railways or rivers and extending away from the central business district. Beyond this were the zones of residence. The outward spread of residences and increasing concentration of jobs, however, could not continue indefinitely, as the strain on transportation facilities became too great to accommodate the gap between home and downtown.

This strain produced a number of results. For example, institutions such as elementary schools followed the population into the suburbs. Selected kinds of retail and service activities, less dependent on accessibility to the entire city market, escaped the growing downtown congestion. These were service stations and grocery and drug stores, for example, which could serve a suburban neighborhood because of the smaller number of customers necessary to sustain their operations. The city and suburbs developed a scattering of such retail outlets. Likewise, new industry found it less and less easy to locate near the city core, as vacant land suitable for industrial use was fast disappearing. There was also decreasing incentive to expand existing industry in the core, not only because of space limitations but also because of rising land costs, growing traffic congestion, and obsolescent facilities. As industry began moving away from the core to other parts of the city and its suburbs, the older centrally located establishments found themselves increasingly unable to compete with the newer, more efficient decentralized plants, thus inducing still greater decentralization.

It was not long, with the availability of the private automobile, before a full scale suburbanization trend was everywhere evident, as activity after activity followed the residential shift toward the city's edge. Entrepreneurs recognized the trend and anticipated suburban growth by establishing large integrated shopping centers and industrial parks. The result was a further acceleration of suburbanization. The outward growth rushed on so fast that the suburbs grew to the detriment of the older central city, increasingly gutted of commercial and industrial activities and finally bombed by urban renewal as a last resort to halt the downward spiral.

In its employment pattern, the city has evolved from a single dominant employment center into a structure in which there is a primary pattern of centers, including the central business district (CBD), which have similar ranges of commercial facilities and services and a secondary distribution of specialized centers of industry, government, education, medicine, or a more limited range of retail and service activities. Even so, the downtown business district continues to be the single most significant organizational node in the urban area.

The suburban shifts have been faster for some urban activities than for others, and consequently there are important differences in the distribution of workplaces for occupational groups. Consider first the differences among the white collar occupations — professional workers, managers, salesmen, and clerical help.

Professional and managerial workers, at the highest levels of socioeconomic status, have two major kinds of workplace locations. The first and historically most important is the central business district. The decline of these white collar jobs downtown has been slower than for nearly any other occupational group. They deal with information and decision making, and more typically require a central access point to make information easily available to clients, consumers of information services, and organizational structures. These occupations serve governments, usually also centrally located. Managerial decisions made at central offices may affect many people in a large area of the city and beyond. Communications, face-to-face contacts, and proximity to large information pools are mandatory. The second significant kind of workplace for professional and managerial workers is in suburban locations. Here those dealing in information serve the industries, institutions, and organizations that occupy the suburbs and require less access to the total information pool. Specialized information production, such as research, may conveniently locate in the suburbs to supply local industry and institutions. Likewise, some research and information processing operations may enjoy a suburban location because they only need access to a limited number of sources for information and ideas. As a result of increasing specialization of knowledge and improving communication, the suburbs are becoming more and more the location for the manufacture, processing, and exchange of information. Added to this are the advantages of the proximity to residential areas in which the professionals and managers live.

Sales workers tend to be fairly widely dispersed throughout the metropolitan area. There is a notable concentration in the central business district, though it has declined in recent decades. There are smaller concentrations sprinkled across the city and suburbs in shopping centers of varying size. The early decentralization of retailing on a store-by-store or neighborhood shopping center basis was enormously intensified by the development of the gigantic, integrated shopping plaza, able to compete favorably with the downtown stores. Thus, salesmen today work in all sections of the urban area but, because of the spatial clustering of many retail stores, their workplaces are concentrated.

Of all the white collar groups, clerical workers are probably the most uniformly distributed within the urban area. All kinds of businesses, institutions, and industries employ clerical help. As with other white collar workers, clerical employees work in greatest numbers in the downtown area. Elsewhere in the city they are seldom employed in huge numbers at a single location, but at a great variety of geographically dispersed activities, and often at the same locations as individuals of other occupational groups.

A sizable majority of clerical workers are female. One subgroup of women are unmarried or in the earliest stages of family development, and tend to live in urban or suburban apartments which may be chosen because of proximity to the workplace. Others are wives helping to augment the income of their more established families. The ubiquitous distribution of clerical jobs allows these women to find employment near their homes, which in turn have usually been selected because of convenience to the husband's job.

Craftsmen-foremen and operatives are in the upper

socioeconomic half of the four blue collar occupational groups. They are skilled workmen in many different trades (including the construction workers employed in urban renewal and suburban expansion) and foremen over other workers. Although in occupational prestige they are considered below clerical workers, they often enjoy considerably higher incomes. Craftsmen-foremen, not unlike the clerical group, have a city-wide distribution of employment opportunities. Operatives, who are skilled and semi-skilled factory workers, work wherever industry is concentrated. Neither group is particularly numerous in the city's central business district; both, in fact, have become increasingly decentralized with the suburbanization of industry.

The only blue collar group that has a fairly large percentage of workplaces downtown is service workers. However, with the exception of the low-income residential area near the downtown, service workers are employed in large numbers throughout the urban area.

Laborers, unskilled workers, have experienced the greatest suburbanization of their workplaces of all the occupational groups. At one time virtually all unskilled jobs were found in the city itself, but with the rapid peripheral urban growth of the last two or three decades laborers have been needed in larger numbers ever farther from the city core near which most of them reside. A serious cost-time burden is thus placed on their ability to travel to work.

Patterns and Problems of Linking Home and Work

Time was when travel patterns in getting between home and work were rather simple. Nearly everyone worked in or near the city center and lived at a distance away depending on social status. Virtually all traffic focused on the downtown, like ants to an ant hill. In those days, the effort required in getting to work depended on where one lived, and in the earliest period of city growth, as indicated above, it was the high status individuals who most likely lived closest to the downtown work cluster. The poor not only often worked longer hours but took longer in getting to work. Today the metropolis displays a confusing complexity of travel patterns in its attempt to connect the ever-shifting location of homes and workplaces. How has such an untidy pattern of dashing to and fro developed and what are its implications for the several occupational groups?

As pointed out before, the city attempted to adjust its residential space on the basis of social preferences and hostilities. However, transportation technology at first changed too rapidly for social stability to reach its spatial equilibrium. The streetcar and commuter railroad led to the development of an outer ring, within the city, of middle-income households, leaving the rich and the poor in tight spatial juxtaposition. Then, with differential automobile ownership, a temporary balance was achieved between space and status when the high-status group created the first suburban ring, and work-trip length was generally greater the higher the status. All jobs were still primarily in the central business district or in the adjacent wholesaling-manufacturing sector. Those of higher status, although traveling farther, could do so in a reasonable period of time by private automobile or the commuter railroad. The poor, unable to afford the automobile, lived near their work; the middle-income were intermediate.

Then came the real beginning of decentralization in workplaces and the nice balance began to teeter. Among the first jobs to decentralize were those in selected industrial activities which manufactured less bulky materials and required greater proportions of craftsmen-foremen and operatives than unskilled workers. Such industries could rely on the motor truck to handle the materials used in processing, as well as the relatively high value finished products. Salesmen and clerical workers also found a growing demand for their services in outlying areas. The middle-income occupations, following their jobs in the now ubiquitous automobile, took up residence increasingly in the suburbs and formed the second suburban ring. The pattern of work-trips remained focused on the downtown, especially for the high status workers; the lowest status group continued to live near the older downtown industrial and other employment centers.

Finally, the precarious balance between living and social space, in part eroded by the decentralization of middle-income employment, became almost fully destroyed by the outward spread of jobs for both the rich and the poor. The higher status households migrated to the suburbs, establishing the third suburban ring, but found themselves, on the average, no farther from their workplaces, which followed them to the suburbs. The suburban job potential for professional and managerial workers merely sped up the prevailing trend. For the lower status occupations, a serious transportation hurdle stood between home and work locations. Concentrated residentially in the central city, low-income workers found themselves chasing fewer and fewer jobs farther and farther into suburbia.

As long as workplace location maintained its downtown permanency, it became possible — given a long enough period of residential adjustment — for the living and social space to correspond. Work-trip length varied rather directly with social status. When the place of work, however, underwent geographical shifts, groups at the two extremes of

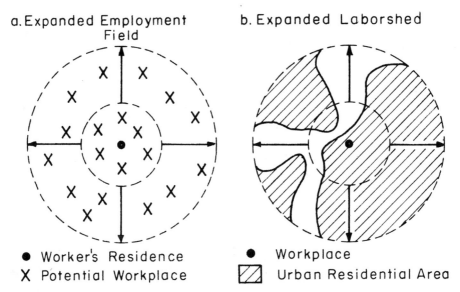

a. Expanded Employment Field

b. Expanded Laborshed

● Worker's Residence   ● Workplace

X Potential Workplace   ▨ Urban Residential Area

Figure 3.3: The expansion of potential workplaces (Figure 3.3a) for one remaining at the same residence with an improvement in transport technology; and the potential increase of residential choice for a worker remaining at the same place of work as transportation improves (Figure 3.3b).

the status scale had to travel the longest distances to get to work. The present trend, the reversal of the old association between distance traveled and social status, seems to point toward the time when the rich will live closest to their work and the poor the farthest — unless public policy intervenes to provide low cost homes in the suburbs.

Three categories of commuting now characterize the urban community. There remains, first of all, the downtown journey to work, in which trips originating in the suburbs and city focus on the historic central core. The modern urban freeway system and the often not-so-modern public transit service are structured primarily to serve such traffic. Both of these transportation systems have been built not merely as a service to downtown workers but at the same time to serve shoppers in an attempt to strengthen and maintain the downtown as a competitive core. A second category is "reverse commuting," in which those living in the city work in the suburbs, traveling in the reverse direction from the downtown worker. An automobile is mandatory for such trips, since transit facilities are seldom geared in scheduling or routing to reverse commuting. The third pattern is "lateral commuting." These work-trips involve movement within the city and suburbs in which the primary direction is neither toward the downtown or toward the periphery. Lateral commuting, both over long and short distances, focuses on the growing multitude of scattered workplaces. While public transit is usually inadequate to facilitate reverse commuting, it is virtually nonexistent for lateral movement in the urban area.

To understand more fully the basis for these three commuting patterns, one needs to appreciate the increasing levels of personal mobility over the last three-quarters of a century. Fundamental changes have occurred in location of residences and employment; these changes have been in part the result of the improved ease of traveling about the urban area. They have also been related to its opposite: urban travel congestion.

Take a single worker residentially located at any given place in the city. Surrounding his residence there exists a potential "employment field" or area in which he may conveniently travel to a workplace. For a given occupational type, the worker may have several alternative job locations within the employment field. Beyond some particular limit, the time, effort, and costs of daily traveling will become too burdensome if he is to maintain the same residence. If the burden of traveling is very great, his employment field will be restricted. Historically, the urban worker has enjoyed a continuously expanding employment field. Figure 3.3a illustrates the geographical expansion of a hypothetical employment field. The net impact of greater mobility is increased choice of where to work. When multiplied over the entire urban work force, transport technology has meant that workers may choose to retain their residence and seek workplaces at greater and greater distances away from home at little or no added effort. The higher status family has always had a larger employment field and a greater choice not only in where to work but also in where to live, compared to the typical low-income household.

An analogous concept to the employment field, but related to the location of an employment center, is the laborshed, or the area from which workers can be conveniently drawn to work at a particular place (Fig. 3.3b). Mobility has seen the expansion of the laborshed, from the era in which one could go only as far as he could walk or travel by animal, to modern automobile commuting distances. The growth in laborsheds has allowed a single workplace to attract labor from ever wider areas of the metropolis. From the point of view of the worker, the larger laborshed grants greater freedom of choice in where to live while retaining the same workplace.

Thus the consequence of the areal enlargement of both the laborshed and the employment field is reflected in three commuting patterns discussed above. The downtown laborshed has spread as fast and as far as the periphery of the urban area has diffused into the countryside. The central business district has been able to draw workers from all parts of the metropolitan area (usually in approximate proportion to the population density). Downtown commuter trips have become longer in length but not necessarily in travel time. It is clearly the higher status occupations that chiefly benefit by being able to reside in the country club atmosphere of the suburbs, rich in living amenities, and still work downtown. Reverse commuting has resulted from the labor requirements not met from the suburbs being pulled out of the central city. The laborshed for such trips is typically elongated along a particular urban sector and is more restricted in size than the downtown laborshed. It is still uncommon for a high percentage of work-trips to originate, say, in a northern sector and terminate at a location in the south of the city. The downtown, with its considerable congestion, acts as a strong deterrent. Although displaying a great deal of variability in size, laborsheds characterized by a predominance of lateral commuting tend to be relatively small, as the main traffic arteries feed into and out of the city core. Circumferential interstate highways, however, are making possible some growth in across-the-city commuting.

Laborsheds and employment fields may have different shapes because of congestion and competition. An idealized circular employment field or laborshed, for example, may in reality be truncated where traffic congestion reaches unreasonable limits. One can simply go farther in the same amount of time in certain directions than in others in the urban area, as streets and traffic permit. Laborsheds may be elongated away from the direction of principal competition from other employment centers. The shape and configuration of laborsheds will nearly always be · modified by the particular residential distribution of the different occupational groups composing the labor force.

As noted before, the long-term trend has been for distance to exert a smaller and smaller influence on travel behavior, a condition true of all status groups but one in which the high prestige group has maintained an obvious advantage. While technology in transportation has increased urban mobility, the congestion achieved by each upward lift has, as it were, reduced this rise by a congestion factor. The friction in moving through urban space comes much more from the movement of others through the same space than it does from distance itself.

Rural to Urban Linkages

It is therefore not surprising that the combination of traffic congestion in the city and the potential for easy movement over uninhabited space has produced a fair number of urbanites who live in the countryside rather far from the city to which they are economically and socially tied. The United States Bureau of the Census classifies such people as "rural nonfarm," since they are not significantly engaged in agriculture and yet live in the rural rather than the built-up urbanized area. In 1960 the rural nonfarm population in the United States was 40 million, and by 1970 had grown to 43 million, accounting for over 21 percent of the pop-

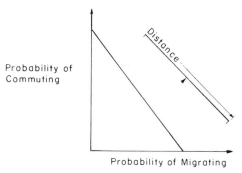

Probability of
Commuting

Probability of Migrating

Figure 3.4: The decision whether to migrate to a city from a rural area or to commute to that city depends upon the distance the individual is from the city, greater distances increasing the probability that one will migrate rather than commute. From James O. Wheeler, "Commuting and the Rural Nonfarm Population," *Professional Geographer*, Vol. 23, April, 1971, p. 120.

ulation. Despite their census designation, these people are basically part of the urban population, as they work, shop, and visit in the city just like any other urban household. The only real difference is that these folk prefer a rural residence. They are the frontiersmen of the urban domain.

Consider a single city offering employment surrounded by a declining agricultural region. The rural resident forced out of agriculture by declining profits will have two choices: migrating to the city or commuting to urban employment. Under what conditions will he prefer one over the other? Assuming no strong sentimental identification with the land, the decision will be based on a trade-off between the relative housing costs at the urban versus the rural location and the cost or effort perceived in commuting to the urban center. Since the housing costs in the rural area should not vary geographically in any regular manner, one may consider the relative housing cost to be a constant in decision making. Therefore, distance to the employment center, measured in travel costs and effort, is a paramount factor.

The overall relationship between migration and commutation may be summarized in Figure 3.4. The decision whether to migrate or commute to the city depends on the distance involved, a greater distance lending a higher probability to migration because of the increasingly onerous transport effort of daily commuting. Conversely, at a short distance the economic justification for migration is weaker and the commutation burden is less intensely felt. Thus at a great distance from the city, under the assumptions of a single employment alternative and declining agriculture, most households will migrate and a very few heads of households will commute to the city; but as distance becomes shorter an increasingly higher proportion of heads of house will prefer to commute. At a given distance, A, which may be called a *critical isotim*, migration will become dominant and substituted for commuting.

The relationship between migration and commuting may also be viewed in historical context (Figure 3.5). In phase one, owing largely to limited transport technology, migration to the urban employment center occurs whenever there is a labor surplus in the agricultural area that can

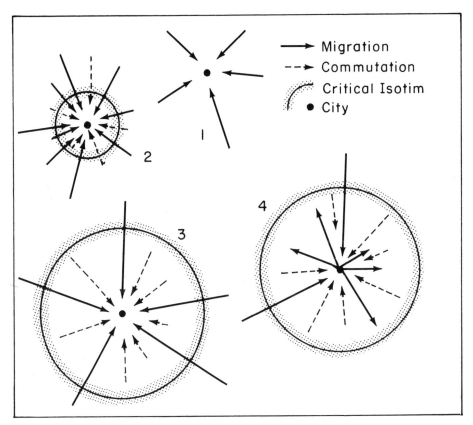

Figure 3.5: Four phases of urban development. First cities grow because of in-migration. Secondly some short distance commuting takes place, but the geographic extent of it is small (critical isotim). The third phase sees an increase in long distance work trips, and finally the last stage has in-migration slowing down but out-migration from the city to the rural fringe greatly accelerating. From Wheeler, see Figure 3.4, p. 121.

be utilized in the city. Phase two depicts short distance commuting, as initial transport improvements permit, and continued migration from throughout the region of agricultural decline. By phase three, the critical isotim, setting the limits of the city's laborshed, has been pushed much farther away from the city, and longer work-trips have become correspondingly more common. In the last phase, urban to rural migration is superimposed on phase three, adding an even greater number of commuters to the rural nonfarm category, and the relative importance of rural to urban migration is reduced. Thus, rural to urban migration has been gradually replaced by commuting, and in phase four, best representing post-World War II conditions, urban to rural migration has made the longer journey to work even more common.

The rural nonfarm population consists of two groups: commuters left as residuals by the migration process and recent urban to rural migrants who prefer rural living and city working. It follows that these two groups would differ in socioeconomic and demographic characteristics. The non-migrant may be less educated, of lower income and occupational status, and older than the urban to rural migrant. The recent migrant to the rural area, at the leading edge of the third suburban ring, may have higher income, occupational status, and educational achievement, as well as being in the earlier stage of the family cycle.

It is not entirely the wealthy, however, who are found in the rural-urban fringe. Just as common is the middle-income family. Take a large family of middle income residing within the urban area. As the city grows in size, lower-income households may encroach upon the middle-income neighborhood. The middle-income family has a choice of changing residence or remaining in what may be perceived as a now undesirable residential location. If there is to be a change in residence, two realistic alternatives are possible: the household may simply move to another middle-income neighborhood or in selected cases the family may elect to reside in the rural area. Two other choices are not likely: moving into a high density area of poorer housing or migrating to an upper-income suburb. The middle-income household with children, not being able to afford the large amount of residential space in a suburban location and refusing to live in a poorer part of town, may choose a rural residence while maintaining urban employment. However, not all middle-income families are equally likely to make the rural residential choice, because of "problems" of schools and shopping.

Only those families which are unusually mobile are willing to substitute the inconvenience of long distance daily commuting for the savings in housing costs associated with the rural environment. The very poorest families cannot afford the substitution, and live close to work. Most of the high-income families prefer suburban living, although many have spilled over into the countryside. Families with relatively youthful, high mobility males earning medium incomes often less concerned about their children's formal education, and frequently keeping pets, are typically found living in the rural fringe. Such families derive considerable psychological utility from the rural life, which is viewed as "a good place to raise children" and "away from the big city hustle and bustle." The rural nonfarm household represents a unique combination of the four basic factors of residential location: income level, social prestige, family structure, and mobility preferences.

The metropolitan area described here might best be visualized in extent by taking a bottle of ink and turning it upside down on a sidewalk, with the ink depicting the extent and outline of the urban area. Then, taking a badly leaking fountain pen, shake and splatter ink all around as the mood of the task dictates. There, before you, you will have the typical American city, flowing outward in irregular spatial profile from the large blob in the center. You will likely have some linear splatters, showing the population lined up along the highways leading into the rural area. And if you have been properly reckless, you will have many dots and splots over a wide area of the sidewalk to represent the scattered rural nonfarm families, who are connected to the urban area through their automobiles and are therefore a functional and geographical part of the metropolis.

Although a psychologist viewing this ink spot might become fixated by the ugliness and lack of symmetry in the pattern, the urbanologist knows the pattern is held together by the functional interdependency of each component part. However, this is not to suggest that our cities have reached their most ideal, efficient, and balanced operating state. We find much about our cities that we would want to change. But if our urban areas do not always behave as we might want them to, it is only the result of our own behavior within them. Individual decisions, multiplied by each other, bring about trends and shifts, for example, in urban residential and employment structure. If residential relocations and workplace growth and migration did not occur so rapidly, these two features of urban space might be brought into closer balance, and the linkages between home and work could become less complicated and the ensuing congestion more tolerable. Planning might catch up with and channel growth, rather than, as now, trail along behind to patch up the landscape assaulted by the march of change. However, change has been the most permanent inhabitant of the city and will not leave. The changes in urban residential and employment geography are profoundly intertwined with the changes in the transportation system which ties together the city's social and economic spaces. To promote urban efficiency through planning is to build those plans on a fundamental foundation of change. And to plan the kind of city we would like to have tomorrow necessitates the deepest insight and understanding of the kind of city we have now and had in the past.

Chapter 4

Transportation
and the Ghetto

Today almost half the black population of the United States is found in fifty urban areas. In five of these cities, blacks make up more than fifty percent of the population (See Table 4.1). The highest proportion is in Washington, D.C., and Compton, California, where seventy-one percent of the population is black. Other large cities with more than fifty percent black population are Newark, New Jersey; Gary, Indiana; and Atlanta, Georgia. Seven other large cities have over forty percent black population; proportions of one-quarter to one-third black populations are fairly typical of many other large cities. If present trends continue, most large cities will become predominantly black in the next generation.

The black population of the United States stands at just over twenty-two million, or slightly more than eleven percent of the nation's total. Starting in this century, especially after World War I and further accelerating after World War II, blacks migrated in large numbers from Southern rural areas to major urban centers, particularly in the industrial North. In 1910 approximately twenty-five percent of the black population was considered urban; by 1970 the same percentage was classified as rural. Sixty percent of the blacks still lived in the South in 1960, but by 1970 only half lived there, as migration to the North and West continued. The highest concentrations of rural blacks remain in the southern states.

Prior to the mass out-migration from the South, most blacks were engaged in agriculture, first as slaves and then mostly as tenants. Few were employed in urban areas. However, in the past half century the switch from the poor rural agriculturalist to the urbanized laborer has not

Table 4.1   Black Population in Major
Politically Incorporated Cities
in the United States

City	Black Population 1970	Total Population 1970	Percentage Black 1970
New York City, N.Y.	1,666,636	7,867,760	21.2
Chicago, Ill.	1,102,620	3,366,957	32.7
Detroit, Mich.	660,428	1,511,482	43.7
Philadelphia, Pa.	653,791	1,948,609	33.6
Washington, D.C.	537,712	756,510	71.1
Los Angeles, Calif.	503,606	2,816,061	17.9
Baltimore, Md.	420,210	905,759	46.4
Houston, Tex.	316,551	1,232,802	25.7
Cleveland, Ohio	287,841	750,903	38.3
New Orleans, La.	267,308	593,471	45.0
Atlanta, Ga.	255,051	496,973	51.3
St. Louis, Mo.	254,191	622,236	40.9
Memphis, Tenn.	242,513	623,530	38.9
Dallas, Texas	210,238	844,401	24.9
Newark, N.J.	207,458	382,417	54.2
Indianapolis, Ind.	134,320	744,624	18.0
Birmingham, Ala.	126,388	300,910	42.0
Cincinnati, Ohio	125,070	452,524	27.6
Oakland, Calif.	124,710	361,561	34.5
Jacksonville, Fla.	118,158	528,865	22.3
Kansas City, Mo.	112,005	507,087	22.1
Milwaukee, Wis.	105,088	717,099	14.7
Pittsburgh, Pa.	104,904	520,117	20.2
Richmond, Va.	104,766	249,621	42.0
Boston, Mass.	104,707	641,071	16.3
Columbus, Ohio	99,627	539,677	18.5
San Francisco, Calif.	96,078	715,674	13.4
Buffalo, New York	94,329	462,768	20.4
Gary, Ind.	92,695	175,415	52.8
Nashville-Davidson, Tenn.	87,851	448,003	19.6
Norfolk, Va.	87,261	307,951	28.3
Louisville, Ky.	86,040	361,472	23.8
Ft. Worth, Texas	78,324	393,476	19.9
Miami, Fla.	76,156	334,859	22.7
Dayton, Ohio	74,284	243,601	30.5
Charlotte, N.C.	72,972	241,178	30.3
Mobile, Ala.	67,356	190,026	35.4
Shreveport, La.	62,152	182,064	34.1
Jackson, Miss.	61,063	153,968	39.7
Compton, Calif.	55,781	78,611	71.0
Tampa, Fla.	54,720	277,767	19.7

Table 4.1 Cont'd.

City	Black Population 1970	Total Population 1970	Percentage Black 1970
Jersey City, N.J.	54,595	260,545	21.0
Flint, Mich.	54,237	193,317	28.1
Savannah, Ga.	53,111	118,349	44.9
San Diego, Calif.	52,961	696,769	7.6

meant, for most blacks, the better life anticipated by the move to the cities. Black migration occurred during a period of industrialization which required growing proportions of skilled and semi-skilled labor. The unskilled jobs that were awaiting the black upon his urban arrival paid poorly. The general lack of educational background and urban employment experiences of the Southern black meant a continued hard life in the North.

The long-standing and well-known racial discrimination in the South was exchanged for a perhaps more subtle, but nonetheless potent kind of discrimination in Northern cities. While in the South traditional black-white communication existed and selected forms of interaction were permissible within the black-white social constraints, in the North blacks found themselves isolated and cut off from the social and economic life of middle-class white society. Interracial contact was relatively infrequent, and racially discriminatory attitudes among whites tended to surface particularly when the "threat" of contact with blacks was immediately perceived.

Although discrimination in employment was a serious factor for the black to contend with, an even more basic and far-reaching problem occurred in the urban housing market. Blacks tended to settle in the oldest, poorest housing areas of the city. Because of continued inmigration and rapid natural increase, these black residential concentrations became densely populated and spilled out into adjacent housing areas. Whites wishing to avoid contact with blacks — fearing the sudden changes in their neighborhood, believing their property values would plummet, and seeing their schools becoming "mixed" — began moving away from what had now clearly developed into a black ghetto. Whites who could afford the housing moved into the suburbs. The vacancies left by the fleeing whites soon became filled by the swelling black population. The small black ghetto in the old section of the city, usually near the downtown area, spread over the ever larger portions of the city.

One area, however, into which very few blacks moved was the suburbs, those separate, incorporated cities which sprang up encircling the old political city, often cutting it off from further areal expansion. The suburbs were of course functionally a part of the political city, as they served as dormitories for white workers who traveled to the city for employment. Even retail and industrial activities dispersed into these suburbs. But not blacks. The result is that more and more modern urban areas have a white suburban ring enclosing the political city that is now or rapidly is becoming predominantly black.

The percentage of blacks who actually moved to the suburbs during the decade 1960 to 1970 was only 4.5 percent, up merely 0.3 percent from the previous decade. Although higher housing costs in the suburbs may be one factor in retarding city to suburban migration, it is by no means the major one, as low-income whites are moving to the suburbs at a much faster rate than blacks. In a recent survey of white attitudes toward black people, two-thirds of the whites interviewed in fifteen cities felt that blacks miss out on good housing because white owners will not sell or rent to them. Discrimination in the urban housing market, despite "open housing" regulations in many cities, remains a primary frustration to blacks seeking alternative housing needs.

Some writers have argued that residential segregation of blacks will follow the classic model of various ethnic groups which became assimilated into society as they rose in socioeconomic status. With assimilation goes residential integration, as foreign-born groups merge imperceptibly into society over a period of one or two generations. As applied to the residential segregation of blacks, however, the classic melting pot model does not quite fit reality. First of all, blacks are much more segregated residentially than any immigrant group has been and this segregation has lasted for a much longer period of time. Not only is racial residential segregation currently more pronounced than ethnic housing segregation, but, more importantly, while segregation of foreign-born groups over the years has declined sharply the segregation of blacks in American cities has actually increased in many cases. Moreover, whereas immigrants with rising incomes could locate outside the ethnic cluster, blacks with high incomes have not been equally as successful in securing housing away from the black ghetto. Although foreign born and blacks may both be able to improve their socioeconomic lot and raise their educational level, the black has not been able to overcome his pigmentation and the stereotypes it generates in the minds of both whites and other blacks.

In spite of a pessimistic past experience in black-white relations, one must look toward the future. The white suburbs are by no means exclusively inhabited by racists. Rather, white Americans are racist by degrees, from the vocal and radical segregationist to the non-discriminatory citizen. Likewise, black attitudes range from the militant black racists to those who judge people on a basis other than skin color. What is desperately needed at this time in the American city is a reduction in racial rancor on all sides. No single approach to this problem or simple single solution can cope with such a complex and many-sided issue. Nevertheless, an understanding of one component of the perplexing urban racial system is a step along the right road. This chapter examines the the transportation needs and opportunities of the black ghetto and the resulting social and economic impact on blacks.

Accessibility and Travel Patterns

The residential segregation of blacks in American cities, a product of long-lasting discrimination, is related to the variety of transportation problems confronting ghetto dwellers. Inadequate transportation, though inseparable from other difficulties of ghetto life, stands as a major barrier to many day-to-day activities, perpetuating isolation and immobility. The fundamental advantage that a city has to offer — lower total communication and transportation costs — is not fully available to the poor who reside in the black ghetto. Blacks are not able to participate completely and equally in the wide range of opportunities and services provided in the urban area. Since opportunities for social and economic contact are geographically dispersed over the metropolitan area, transportation is a key element in the enjoyment of and participation in an urban life style.

It is a major paradox of the twentieth century American cities that blacks reside in or near the most accessible parts of the metropolitan area, and are yet the most immobile of all groups. Figure 4.1 shows accessibility within a medium sized Midwestern city (Lansing, Michigan). Here accessibility refers specifically to ease of movement, or the ease with which one can get from one place in the city to all others. For illustrative purposes, this figure is drawn with lines of equal accessibility as a percentage of the point of highest accessibility, the downtown business district. Thus we see that accessibility, as measured by distance separating places in the city, declines away from the city center, with the most inaccessible locations in the city being in the peripheral suburbs. The more central the location, the more accessible it is.

Looking again at Figure 4.1, one notices the location of the major black ghetto, to the immediate southwest of the central business district. Although occupying a central location, with approximately ninety percent of maximum accessibility, the actual travel behavior of the ghetto dwellers falls drastically short of such an accessibility figure. While the accessibility map describes potential accessibility as derived from location, travel behavior substantiates the actual level of accessibility reflecting day-to-day movement in the city. When measurement of black travel is taken among sixty places in the city, it is found that connectivity among these places is only twelve percent of the maximum connectivity

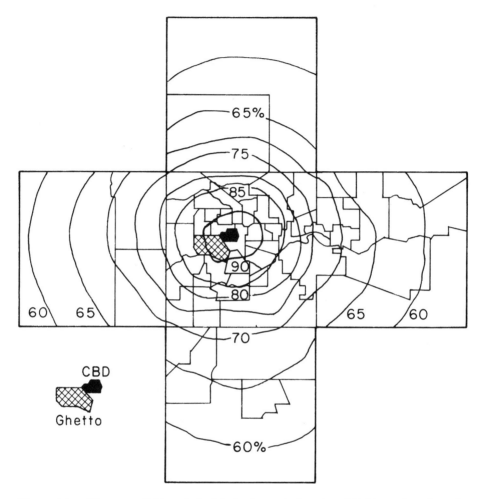

Figure 4.1: The accessibility of the black ghetto in Lansing, Michigan, based on the percentage of maximum accessibility to the city, indicates that blacks are located near the area of maximum accessibility to the city as a whole. In terms of actual travel behavior, however, blacks are very much confined.

possible. In other words, when a black travels between two places in the city, a direct connection is said to exist. All places among which a direct connection exists are compared to all possible direct connections that could exist. The result: an extremely low level of connections among parts of the metropolitan area.

A second step is to find which areas are least connected with the ghetto and which are most closely linked. Not surprisingly, the ghetto is least connected in travel by blacks with distant white suburban and fringe locations. These represent extensive portions of the metropolitan

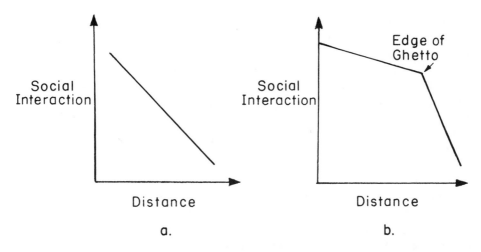

Figure 4.2: The normal distance decline in social interaction with distance (Figure 4.2a). In Figure 4.2b the edge of the ghetto shows a marked break in the intensity of social interaction beyond that point.

area. Even places within the political city of Lansing are by and large poorly tied with the black ghetto. The linkages within the ghetto, however, are noticeably high. In fact, it is as though interaction, being blocked from outside penetration, reaches an astounding intensity for blacks within the ghetto. It is possible to define the ghetto not only on the basis of high density of black population but also by the high intensity of linkages. Connectivity within the ghetto is close to the maximum.

A number of barriers are responsible for the fact that a highly accessible location within the city generates such a small magnitude of actual connections and sends so few trips to the rest of the urban area. On the one hand there are the physical barriers, typical of many urban ghettos. These literally block the ghetto off from its surroundings. They take the form of heavily traveled streets, parks, industrial complexes, hilly terrain, rivers, and more recently urban freeways. These barriers inhibit free movement across them — like buffer zones between feuding political territories. With such barriers, black residential penetration is restricted.

A more powerful barrier to movement is simply "social distance," a barrier in the minds of men. Social distance is an individual's evaluation of his response toward having someone of a different racial, ethnic, or status group live next door, a block away, within the neighborhood, and so on. Social distance preferences lie at the base of all social relations, as well as greatly influencing economic relationships. Since the number of normal contacts generated by one's social communication network decreases with distance away from the individual, those residing at a great geographical distance are often automatically socially removed, in which case an equilibrium exists between social and geographical distance. Such a balance is upset, however, when geographical distance becomes smaller than social distance.

Figure 4.2a shows theoretically the typical decay of social interaction with distance. Here a situation is described in which geographical proximity exactly corresponds to levels of social intimacy. A different pattern of decline in social interaction over distance occurs within the context of the ghetto, however. In Figure 4.2b, there is an overall decrease in interaction with distance — a modest decline within ghetto space and a precipitous plunge beyond the ghetto edge. The sharp break in the pattern of interaction at the boundary of the ghetto indicates a substantial barrier to social communications. If the steeper portion of the line becomes increasingly steeper over time periods, segregation is intensified, implying that interracial ties are becoming weakened. When the line describing interaction becomes straightened with time, the ghetto becomes eroded and ill-defined, with a perfectly straight line measuring the complete disappearance of the ghetto.

It is not only actual social or even economic interaction that abruptly declines at the ghetto boundary. It is also a feeling of comfort, of group identity, in short, a sense of territoriality. The high intensity of social interaction within the ghetto produces a more cohesive and self-sustaining neighborhood, all of which develops a keener sense of territoriality. Because of the physical and social barriers surrounding the ghetto, its inhabitants seek within the ghetto to accumulate social bonds, reinforcing a sense of racial identity imposed by a territorial identity.

Of all the purposes of travel in the city, the trip to work is the most frequent and probably the most basic, as it links the household with its source of income. An immediately apparent problem is posed for the resident of the black ghetto in the large urban center. Whereas the typical white has a flexible locational choice throughout the urban area, in part constrained by distance, the typical black is restricted to a ghetto residence irrespective of his place of employment. Moreover, because of his limited residential choice, his employment choice may be significantly reduced by the high costs of transportation. How many jobs and homes are spread too far? Several years ago, one author estimated that racial segregation in housing "may cost Negroes as many as 35,000 jobs in Chicago and 9,000 in Detroit."[2] At present the situation has probably become even worse.

In the summer of 1968 a "jobmobile" toured ghetto neighborhoods in Philadelphia collecting applications for work. As one businessman who hired a hundred workers found, "the expense and inconvenience of the two hour bus and trolley ride to his suburban electronics plant caused most of the new employees to quit within a few weeks."[3] Such a problem has become more and more typical with the spread of jobs into the suburbs beyond the commuting reach of the ghetto labor force.

Business and industry have been moving to the suburbs at an alarming rate. In the past, there was more pull to the suburbs than push from the older central city, as cheap land was sought convenient to truck transportation. In recent years, evidence is accumulating that movement into the suburbs is driven by the desire to escape the congestion and crime of the central city, as much if not more than because of the attraction of the suburbs. In any case, it is a snowballing process, since more and more development, housing, and people are already in the suburbs, attracting future growth. The Regional Plan Association estimated that the sprawling New York metropolitan area will grow by 2.4 million new jobs by 1985 and that two million of these will be in the suburbs.

Jobs that are moving away to the suburbs most rapidly are those requiring low skills. Blacks consequently are having to chase fewer and fewer manual jobs farther and farther into the suburbs. Statistics show that normally over three-quarters of all low skilled workers do not retain their jobs after the employment site has relocated in the suburbs, in contrast to the more than four-fifths at the executive level who do.[4] The suburban housing shortage for low-income workers is a problem for all workers whose jobs relocate to the suburbs, but the difficulty is most serious for the black who faces not only a housing shortage but also a discriminatory housing market. In many suburbs, zoning regulations preclude the construction of inexpensive homes and subdivisions are divided into large lots to ensure rather widely spaced and more costly housing.

Add to this the problem of mass transportation. Public transit is practically nonexistent in the suburbs. In the few large cities in which transit operates, it is geared to moving commuters downtown, not to the suburbs. Yet thirty-five percent of the residents of central cities do not own an automobile, and the percentage is even higher in parts of the black ghetto. An unknown percent own a vehicle which is so rundown and unreliable as to make the daily trip on the high-speed freeway almost impossible. A resident of Detroit's central city describes why he lost his job at a suburban automobile plant:

> No matter what time I started out for work, it seemed like I couldn't make it on time. It was taking nearly all I made to keep my car running anyway. One week it broke down on the freeway three times and the last time I just left it there, still parked there for all I know.

Over 20,000 cars were abandoned last year in New York City alone.

The low percentage of automobile ownership in the central city in

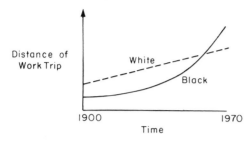

Distance of Work Trip

White

Black

1900   1970

Time

Figure 4.3: The distance for work-trips has increased, owing to transport improvements, for both blacks and whites since about 1900, but in the past several years blacks are often forced to travel farther than whites to reach employment locations which are spreading into suburban and rural fringe areas.

general and in the ghetto in particular means that the highway and freeway system is of primary benefit to those living in the suburbs where two and even three automobiles per household are common. Urban freeways provide easy access to downtown from the suburbs and also encourage crosstown movement, either going through the heart of the city or around the city on the perimeter routes. For a ghetto resident with an automobile, they are equally useful. Without a car, they are a barrier. Some writers and public officials have noted one possible solution: government subsidies for cars for the poor (new Volks for poor folks).

Because of the high cost of auto ownership, many ghetto residents must rely on mass transit, if it exists. Suburban employment locations are highly dispersed, oriented to automobile access. Mass transit can operate economically and efficiently only when population and employment are concentrated in the city, hence its focus on downtown workplaces. Planned expenditures to extend transit farther into the suburbs will not substantially benefit blacks living in ghettos near the downtown. In short, the transportation system of the metropolitan area is not organized to serve the needs of whites and blacks equally, at least as long as housing segregation is the norm.

Historically the black was better off in getting to work than he is today. When the great majority of jobs were centrally located, the black worker found his ghetto fairly conveniently located to his workplace. Until recent years, the average work-trip length for a black was less than for a white worker. Public transit could serve the black about as well as it did the white, who lived somewhat farther from his work. However, with decentralization of employment, the relationship began to change, the change first becoming noticeable in the fifties and early sixties (Figure 4.3).

During this period, data show that the average distance of work-trips for blacks began to increase rather markedly, whereas the length for whites rose at a slower rate corresponding largely to overall transport improvements and efficiencies. Important differences in trip length by occupational status also came to characterize blacks. During the nineteenth and early twentieth century there was little significant variation in trip length by occupational level. With decentralization, however, it was the jobs at the lower end of the occupational scale that diffused suburbanward fastest. The result was a growing separation between home and work for those blacks with low job skills and income — the group least able to afford the transportation costs associated with the greater distance in getting to work.

Just the opposite situation took place among whites. With opportunities for suburban residential amenities, it was the upper-income whites whose separation between suburban residence and downtown employment first exceeded the home-work separation of other income groups. With general decentralization of business, industry, and the white population, shorter travel distances for whites became possible. Said differently, whites have been able to increase their work-trip length in response to transportation improvements; blacks have found their work-trips lengthened not so much by increased levels of mobility reflected in transportation advances as by "forced mobility" imposed on the rather static residential pattern by rapid employment changes. We have a paradox. Although whites in general are considered more mobile than blacks, it is the blacks who register the longest average trips in traveling to work.

Two very informative maps, taken from a study by Professor Deskins of the residence-workplace interaction in Detroit for the years 1953 and 1965, illustrate the basic changes in home-work separation between whites and blacks (Figure 4.4). Deskins computed the mean center of white and black residences and workplaces in a manner similar to that used by the U.S. Bureau of the Census to measure the westward-shifting population center of the United States.[5] He also calculated "standard distances," which show the degree of deviation or spread away from the mean centers. In 1953 workplaces for blacks were more decentralized than black residences, but were both much more centralized than the mean centers for whites. In contrast, whites had a more dispersed residential than employment pattern.

Twelve years later the distribution of employment for blacks had dispersed toward the suburbs more rapidly than their residences. Despite the outward movement of white jobs, the mean center of location of white workplaces in 1965 was still closer to the CBD than was the mean center of residence. Comparing the standard distance measurements, one sees that there was dispersion both of home and work for whites between 1953 and 1965, but jobs decentralized more than did residence for blacks, jobs spread suburbanward, though more slowly than for whites, but there was actually an increased concentration of black residences in 1965. Differences in the standard distances between home and work for whites are rather small, especially for the mid-sixties. A large discrepancy exists for blacks, underlining the transportation problems blacks are increasingly facing. Housing discrimination places an undue burden on

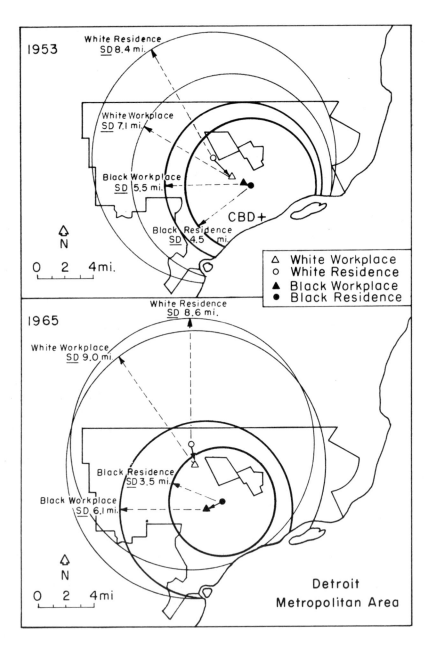

Figure 4.4: The changing relationship between the average location and standard dispersion of residence and workplace for blacks and whites in Detroit, 1953 and 1965. Taken from Donald R. Deskins, Jr., "Residence-Workplace Interaction Vectors for the Detroit Metropolitan Area: 1953 to 1965," in *Interaction Patterns and the Spatial Form of the Ghetto*, Special Publication No. 3, Department of Geography, Northwestern University, 1970, p. 18.

transportation expenditures by blacks, who experience less discrimination in where they may work in the city than in where they may live.

There is evidence that blacks not only bear higher than necessary transportation costs in getting to work but also in carrying out other forms of travel as well. Blacks are typically farther from the new large suburban shopping centers where better item selection is possible and where prices are often lower for the same items than in the ghetto stores, on which higher insurance and often higher rent are charged. Black travel to medical facilities in Chicago likewise is longer than for whites.[6] Sufficient hospital space is often not found in or near the ghetto, and many white physicians have followed their higher paying patients away from the black area.

Freeway Penetration

Highway construction entered a new era in this country in 1956 with the beginnings of the more than 42,000 miles of interstate system. Largely financed (ninety percent) through Federal funding, the limited access system of freeways is designed to link the major cities from one end of the country to the other. Freeways also cut through the urban areas themselves, serving intra- as well as inter-urban movement. It has been within the cities that construction has faced its greatest problems. It is not that the costs of construction are prohibitively high, though the costs do average several million dollars for each mile. Rather, it is that the urban freeways have harmful as well as beneficial impacts on people, institutions, businesses, and social activities.

By placing massive transport arteries around, through, and across cities, extremely far-reaching changes are set into motion, whose ultimate consequences are still unknown. Major readjustments are felt in the travel behavior of a large number of people. Remote locations suddenly become accessible, and formerly accessible places find themselves cut off and isolated from the city as a whole. Changes are initiated in the geographical pattern of commercial, industrial, and residential land use. Fortunes are made and investments are lost in the wake of the spreading urban freeway.

In the initial planning for the construction of the urban freeways, probably no one anticipated the emerging concern and opposition among sizable segments of the people to proposals for the new transportation facility. One thing was for sure, and almost everywhere recognized: The urban freeway would benefit people differently. There arose many opposing positions and viewpoints. Conflicts were perceived between national and local policy, between the needs for increased mobility and the goal of neighborhood stability, between regional needs and local desires, between community participation in decision making and efficiency, decisiveness, and overall planning strategy. The side effects of freeway construction have come to be seen as significant and not always in harmony with the desire to provide safe, efficient, and economical mobility.

About 6,000 miles of urban freeways have been planned but are yet to be constructed. Expressway projects have been delayed or halted in many cities. Although cities everywhere need improved transportation, many people expect to be hurt by freeway construction, especially those whose homes and businesses lie in the direct path of the freeway. What role should community needs and values play in freeway location? Who speaks for the community? Where does transportation rank among community needs and values? What are both the short- and long-run implications of the locational decision for the freeway?

There is very little vacant land available in the central cities. There is almost none of this vacant land available in the swaths of linear dimensions necessary for freeway construction. Transportation planners have been forced to turn to land currently in some other use to acquire freeway right of way. They must reconcile the overall layout of the freeway system with these existing patterns of land use. Given the need for a route from, say, the west to move traffic downtown, what specific route will be chosen and what stands in the path of the freeway? It is here that a large part of the opposition to freeway expansion generates its force.

In a sizable number of American cities, minority groups in particular have developed serious opposition to proposed freeway routing. Blacks have found freeways cutting across their neighborhoods, literally disrupting and destroying their communities. Planners have attempted to justify routing through ghettos as a means of reducing right-of-way costs, since deteriorating ghetto housing is less expensive to acquire than is commercial, industrial, and institutional land. Blacks often regard the freeway as primarily serving the mobility needs of white suburban residents at the expense of the stability of innercity neighborhoods, which are either physically displaced or fragmented by freeway routing.

A proposed freeway through the innercity is frequently seen as a threat to the residents' precarious economic resources and to their valued sense of community and territorial control. Even though the housing destroyed by freeway construction may have been substandard, it is often the only housing the families had been able to afford. Those displaced by the freeway are not always able to obtain housing near their former homes, and social and economic ties, including jobs, are broken. Members of minority groups, such as blacks, achieve personal identity not so much through the powerful institutional units largely controlled by the white majority as they do through the social network within their own neighborhood. This social fabric is pulled apart by freeway construction.

The urban freeway clearly serves differently the mobility needs of various social and racial groups in the city. High-income suburban residents not only have access to jobs and entertainment in the downtown business core but also they have ready connections to most other suburban locations, especially via circumferential freeway links. In contrast, the ghetto resident undertaking social travel must rely largely on the traditional street pattern in carrying out his multi-directional travel. Although one may argue that the ghetto resident is equally as able to utilize a freeway as is his suburban counterpart, the lack of automobile ownership in the central city seriously restricts freeway utilization, whether to gain access to the growing suburban job market and the large suburban shopping centers or simply to move about the city for social purposes.

Part of the problem in freeway planning has to do with the unequal distribution of political clout in our society. More than half the ghetto residents are too young to vote. Community groups seldom are effective, articulate, or even organized. Powerlessness becomes deeply rooted in a negative self-concept, manifested as hopelessness. Resentment deepens when residents feel that the freeway boring through the ghetto has been superimposed by others for their own advantage, destroying the stability of the black neighborhood in order to maintain the stability of suburban communities and to promote the mobility of suburban residents. Frustration develops when the people of the ghetto realize that they do not have an input to decisions which affect them.

Not only does the freeway affect different groups differently but also groups will have different value systems with respect to freeway benefits and disadvantages. Attitudes are molded by the lines of communication available to the individual. If the communication network is directed inward, as with ghetto residents as well as many professional planners, attitudes become solidified around the available but limited information base. In addition, groups face different pressures and perceive different choices open to them. The net result is that ghetto residents place less value on mobility compared with suburban residents. Although both groups highly value community stability, their perception of this stability is very different and the choices open to these two groups vary. For blacks, a sense of social community, personal identity, and a feeling of territorial security are of greater importance than for white suburbanites. Yet, for blacks these are exactly the things most directly threatened by freeway construction.

Beyond the mobility-stability conflict, there is the problem of national versus local policy. These stresses are felt most acutely in the ghetto of the innercity. The automobile majority in society supports a national policy of interstate highways extending across the country. Strong support also exists for improved urban transportation, which translates for most people into highway, not transit, improvement. There are fewer and fewer places in the city that can be reached by transit, whereas with the automobile everyplace becomes accessible. Since local government is generally too weak politically to initiate large scale transportation systems and too weak financially to support even a modest level of highway construction, national policy has been superimposed on the city, and federal financing has carried the lion's share of the cost. Local policy and community values, when in conflict with wider political interest, become ignored or trampled, especially in the politically soft underbelly of the central city. While local pressure groups in the more affluent suburbs can organize and generate strong opposition to a proposed freeway link through newspaper headlines or through direct pressure on the small suburban municipality, blacks and others in the innercity tend to be less organized and effective when confronting a city bureaucracy representing several million people, compared to perhaps several thousand in a suburb. Further, although the freeway may affect nearly everyone in the small suburb (creating nearly unanimous opposition), freeway penetration through the central city affects only a part of a much larger area.

An indirect effect of national policy favoring automobility has been to encourage low density suburban development. It has been argued that if the billions of dollars spent for freeway construction had been spent instead on efficient and effective transit facilities there would have been much less rushing to the suburbs and much less deterioration in the high density central city. Extensive freeway construction, when viewed in this light, has probably favored the higher-income households who have been most able to take advantage of the freeway over low-income blacks who have not found it as useful. Moreover, blacks are largely confined to the area most affected by freeways which have spread out the affluent population and have left a deteriorating urban environment with a shrinking tax base. Thus blacks often feel that they achieve fewer of the benefits while bearing higher community costs and sacrifices.

Despite the harmful effects of freeway penetration of innercity ghettos, there are certain effects that are positive. For those who own a car, travel to the expanding suburban job market is made easier. With the development of public and low cost housing in suburban areas, the freeway is a link between central city and suburban jobs and social areas. If open housing were to become a reality, freeway benefits could be widely enjoyed throughout the urban areas. Finally, it is primarily in the short run that differences between social costs on the one hand and social benefits on the other are significantly at variance. In the long run the social sacrifices necessitated by freeway construction through populated communities become slowly replaced by advantages gained by the accumulated use of the transportation facility.

Several positive signals are beginning to appear on the horizon, as transportation planners are coming to recognize the total impact of the freeways. The past emphasis strictly on user benefits for new transportation systems is starting to give way toward greater regard for nonuser effects. Social and economic consequences of freeways are occupying a greater role in the transportation planning process. Greater sympathy is given to participation by affected citizens in transport decisions. Greater concern is being expressed for environmental quality aspects of freeways and for ways to reduce air pollution through highway planning. Recognition is increasingly given to resolving the conflict between the creation of traffic on freeways and the livability of areas near the freeway. None of these problems, however, is simple, or their solutions would have been discovered a long time ago.

We have learned how to build freeways to the highest engineering specifications, to stack freeway on freeway, and to tunnel beneath the city. But we have yet to learn how to mesh the human social system with the man-made concrete system. "Social engineering" is in its infancy. The delays so widely experienced in recent freeway construction may simply reflect the huge gap in our knowledge between highway engineering and social engineering. Progress in the former may await progress in the latter in order to narrow the gap. Scholars of the city have perhaps too often neglected to ask the inhabitants what kind of city they want to live in. Many inhabitants of our cities, it is true, may not know what they want, but they do know what kind of city they don't like. We have guaranteed that everyone has a freeway to drive on, even though we have not guaranteed that everyone has a car to drive or a decent house to live in. Transportation policy makers, in their ebullience to find modern man's salvation, have quickly found that there are indeed unknown impacts of the transportation system upon the urban environment, the community, and the structure of city growth and change.

Transportation and communication problems are interwoven with all of the serious issues confronting life in the ghetto. Although solution of the transportation problems will not magically cure the ghetto of its ailments, any attempt to improve ghetto life must take into account the role of transportation. Creation of jobs is no solution if the jobs are too far away. Low cost housing is no panacea if located away from jobs, shopping, and recreation, particularly for families with no automobile. Equally important, sources of information only slowly diffuse into the ghetto from outside, during which time the information may become distorted, out-of-date, and meaningless. Likewise, information originating within the ghetto only haltingly seeps outward, where it may be misunderstood, if not ignored. The development of firm, explicit, and meaningful communication between blacks and whites in the city is a necessary but not sufficient condition for improving the quality of life in the ghetto.

At a distant perspective, one is apt to think of the ghetto in a generalized fashion. The need to simplify complex problems through generalization, however, should not lead to the erection of mental stereotypes, where simple-simon solutions are superimposed on real-world situations, leading to the destruction of both. To speak of mobility needs of the ghetto glosses over the problem that these needs are highly variable within ghetto space. Not everyone is equally immobile, nor equally threatened or benefited by an urban freeway. Although solidarity of social interaction does not characterize the black and white populations in general, a wide range of specific and individual interaction patterns do exist. Many writers in describing black Americans have emphasized the lower-income black population, which is predominant, without noting the broad range of incomes within the group.

The most apparent example in American cities today of lifestyle differences reflected in a separate geographical space is the black ghetto, set off from the rest of the metropolitan area. In developing, maintaining, and altering this basic racial feature of the city, transportation and communication take both a direct and indirect role, and are a cause as well as an effect. It should be kept in mind there are at least four salient influences that have lead to the black lifestyle patterns and the separate geographical space in which they are carried out, all operating within the matrix of urban transportation and interaction. These forces are poverty, African origin, Southern heritage, and subjection to Negrophobia.

References

1. Angus Cambell, *White Attitudes Toward Black People* (Ann Arbor: Institute for Social Research, University of Michigan, 1971).

2. John F. Kain, *The Effect of the Ghetto on the Distribution and Level of Nonwhite Employment in Urban Areas* (Santa Monica, California: RAND Corporation Bulletin, P- 3059-1, 1965) p. 18.

3. Richard W. Epps, "Suburban Jobs and Black Workers," *Philadelphia Federal Bank Business Review*, 1969, pp. 3 - 13.

4. *The New York Times*, February 28, 1971.

5. Donald R. Deskins, Jr., "Residence-Workplace Interaction Vectors for the Detroit Metropolitan Area: 1953 to 1965," in *Interaction Patterns and the Spatial Form of the Ghetto*: Evanston, Illinois: Department of Geography, Northwestern University, Special Publication No. 3, 1970, pp. 1 - 23.

6. Richard L. Morrill, Robert J. Earickson, and Philip Rees, "Factors Influencing Distances Traveled to Hospitals," *Economic Geography*, Vol. 46, April, 1970 pp. 161 - 171.

Chapter 5

Communication Costs and Urban Industrial Location

Without manufacturing industry, cities still would be rather small agricultural service centers, acting as markets for the sale and distribution of agricultural products and as retail centers to supply goods and services to the nearby population. These market and retail functions would not require the emergence of cities the size of our present metropolitan areas. In fact it would be nearly impossible to conceive of cities with more than a million people, of which there are now thirty-three in the United States and three each in Canada and Mexico, if it were not for manufacturing activity. Even the great cities of the past were small by modern standards, Rome reaching perhaps a half-million, and Constantinople possibly equalling this total several centuries later. Nashville, Tennessee, and Tulsa, Oklahoma, for example, now equal the population of these classic cities at their peaks of greatness.

Indeed, no city in the world reached a million people until the Industrial Revolution, at which time no more than fifty cities had over 100,000 inhabitants. The Industrial Revolution began in England and adjacent countries across the North Sea, and in the early nineteenth century its impact was strikingly seen in the sudden rise in urban population. London became the first city to surpass a million inhabitants. Based on coal, iron, the steam powered factory, and the railroad, industrial technology brought a flood of people into the city. Ever since, urbanization and industrialization have gone hand in hand. New manufacturing employment has generated the need for a larger urban population, and large cities have in turn attracted new manufacturing enterprises.

The symbiotic relationship between urbanization and industrialization is of course based on the fact that manufacturing locates almost exclusively in cities. For most types of processing cities possess locational advantages not found in rural areas. Locational advantages are directly translatable into dollars and cents, since each location has a given level of cost associated with assembling materials, processing or fabricating them, and distributing the product to market. The sum of these costs for most industries is lower in urban than non-urban locations, and frequently the larger the metropolitan area the greater are the cost savings.

Urbanization economies, the savings a firm enjoys because of an urban location, result from the opportunity to share a variety of urban services with other firms, businesses, and people. A typical firm will require a water supply, fire protection, a labor force, sewage facilities, transportation service and facilities, and commercial and financial services. The possibility for sharing the cost of these services exists in an urban area, whereas all of the services and facilities would have to be provided by the firm itself if it were located in a remote rural area. Put differently, a firm with the same production output would enjoy a lower average cost per item manufactured in an urban than in a nonurban location. Furthermore, in many cases the average cost of a manufactured item will become lower as the city gets larger, hence the tendency for concentration of manufacturing in the larger metropolitan areas.

A second factor, having to do with savings in transportation costs, also favors the agglomeration of industries in cities. When many industries buy and sell products with one another, it makes sense that they all locate relatively nearby. Most manufacturing firms process material that has already undergone some previous processing; only a small minority of industry now process raw materials. Since successive stages of production are required for more and more finished products, the advantages lie with the location of these stages fairly close together to save transportation costs. A large metropolitan area has the diversity necessary to carry out the various processing stages, at the same time substantially reducing overall transfer costs of shipping the materials from one plant to another. A complex web of industrial linkages characterizes large urban areas.

Declining Role of Transportation Costs

Despite the importance of these industrial linkages within metropolitan areas, transportation costs have become of decreasing importance as a factor in industrial location in general.[1] Industry has

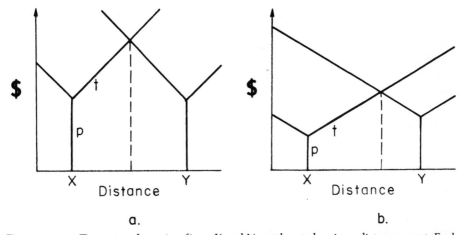

a.   b.

Figure 5.1a: Two manufacturing firms X and Y, are located a given distance apart. Each firm has identical production cost, indicated by p, and like transportation cost, shown by the rise in t with distance away from the firms. The dashed line, depicting the market division, is at an equal distance between the two firms.

Figure 5.1b: The same two firms, with lowered production and transportation cost. However, firm X has lower production cost than firm Y. Therefore, the market division moves to the right to the advantage of X and at the expense of Y.

become more footloose and may locate with orientation to other cost factors. One factor of growing significance is quality of transportation service. More and more firms have become sensitive to service quality, and attempt to find the fastest and most reliable transport service available, rather than the lowest cost transport alternative.

However, the cost of transportation in the past definitely exerted a powerful influence on the location of industry. For example, the iron and steel industry located in Pittsburgh to be near the coalfields because of the large amount of coal then required to produce a ton of pig iron. Reducing the cost of shipping coal was a critical locational goal of the industry, whereas the lower per ton inputs of iron ore could be moved greater distances via the Great Lakes at a relatively low cost. The early manufacturing centers today continue to attract new industry, though not primarily because of their present transportation advantage.

When overland transportation was based on muscle power, its cost was extremely high. Likewise, the average cost of producing an item was high. The manufacturing firm was limited in the area to which it could market its product by high transport costs, and these high costs meant a rather small market area and rather low total sales volume. The firm was not able to take advantage of savings that would have been possible with a larger operation. Figure 5.1a depicts the cost situation for two firms, X and Y, making the same product. The cost, P, describes the expense involved in processing the good; the cost, t, represents the addition of the high transport charge onto the production cost. The line, t, then shows the price of the item as it increases over distance away from production points X and Y. In this example, both firms share the market equally, assuming the demand for the product is evenly spread out with distance.

With the reduction in transport cost brought about by the railroad in the middle nineteenth century, the market reach of any firm suddenly increased. This allowed firms to expand their scale of operations in order to serve the wider sales area. As firms grew larger, the average cost of production went down. Moreover, technological innovations in the production process were now encouraged by the expanding market, leading to further reductions in average costs. In Figure 5.1b, firms X and Y have enjoyed reduced transportation and production costs, but firm X, because of better location on the transport system, has had greater reductions in transport cost. This cost advantage over firm Y is expressed in an enlarged market area, permitting further per unit savings in processing costs. The market area division, illustrated by the dashed line, has moved farther away from X at the expense of Y. As transport costs were reduced over a broad area, firms no longer had to depend on local markets or local sources of material supply. Local monopolies, in the past protected by the high cost of transport, became eroded, and high cost producers, unable to compete, went out of business. Firms with the most favored locations on the transport network survived and thrived, as did firms run by skillful entrepreneurs. Advantageous positions on the transport routes almost inevitably corresponded to urban locations.

The best location for a given manufacturing plant depended on the relative pull of the market and the raw material. If considerable weight was lost during the processing of the raw material, it made good business sense to locate processing close to the source of the material to avoid hauling waste. If weight was added in processing, as with beer, a market location was required. Likewise, a raw material that was highly perishable, such as tomatoes, could not be shipped long distances before being processed, and canning factories went to the tomatoes. On the other hand, industries producing perishable final products, such as bakeries, could not locate very far away from their markets. Thus, industries tended to develop at two principal types of locations: (1) at or near markets, which were generally urban locations and (2) at or near raw material sites, which led to the growth of cities at these locations.

A third type of location for industry was also of some importance. This was at a natural transshipment or break-of-bulk point. When material had to be handled in transferring from one transport carrier to another, say from an ocean vessel to a railroad, it often was economical to process the material at the transshipment point and send on the finished goods to the market. Port cities acted as the principal transshipment points, and consequently grew very rapidly. All major cities in the United States, until the past fifteen years or so, have been located on an ocean, lake, or navigable river.

If the nineteenth century can be characterized as a period of declining transportation costs, the twentieth century has been a time of stabilizing and rising transport costs.[2] During the 1800s, industry tended to concentrate at favored locations, and a region in which most U.S. manufacturing took place became imprinted on the landscape. This belt of industrial concentration extended roughly from Boston, Massachusetts, and Washington, D.C., westward to Milwaukee, Wisconsin, and St. Louis, Missouri. The cities in this region grew rapidly, and industries came to specialize in certain locations because of transportation advantages for materials or for finished products. A national market could now be reached from a single manufacturing location, as with rubber production in Akron and farm machinery in Peoria. Chicago became the meat producing center because of access to livestock and the possibility of shipping meat by refrigerated car.

During the early decades of the twentieth century, transport cost stabilized with respect to other costs. Therefore the role of transportation in the location of new and expanding industry took a back seat to other costs more highly variable from place to place. More industry began to shift from processing raw materials to processing previously manufactured items, loosening the ties of industry with raw material sources.

In recent decades transport costs have risen compared to other costs. This rise, along with other changes in the structure of transportation costs, led to a strong trend toward market locations. The general increase in freight rates encouraged an industry to locate near its market. During this period, population and manufacturing spread to certain parts of the West and South. Since approximately 1929, industry has grown more rapidly in the West and South than in the traditional Northeastern manufacturing region. Particularly, industries with high freight costs have been most likely to decentralize from the Northeast to follow the market. The geographic pattern of a growing number of industries has spread out to correspond to the distribution of population.

In addition to the general rise in transportation cost, several other related factors are responsible for the trend toward market location, or location within large metropolitan areas. There has been a widening gap between the freight rates charged on raw materials and on finished products, with the latter increasing at a more rapid pace. In order to avoid these high shipping costs on manufactured goods, firms are locating near their markets and are willing to pay the lower rate for assembling the raw materials at the market site. Transportation cost for long hauls has grown faster than the cost for short hauls. This is because of technological reductions in terminal or handling costs. Since the cost of actually moving the freight has increased, the cost of short hauls has decreased relative to freight hauls of greater length. There has also been a relative cost shift in favor of shipping small quantities. In the past, there was considerable incentive for a shipper to send large amounts over long distances. Now the advantages of larger consignments have been reduced relative to the less-than-carload shipments. All of these factors, to say nothing of labor supply, favor the location of manufacturing in metropolitan areas, or at market locations. The large urban areas in this country are becoming similarly diversified in industrial composition as the growing local metropolitan market attracts new and expanding industry.

Most of the above changes in the structure of transportation costs are the result of the motor truck. The truck is a more expensive form of transportation than the railroad, and the growth of truck transportation has contributed to the general increase in cost of freight movement. But the truck gives small shippers an opportunity to send their products to market, in contrast to the railroad, which is most economical for large carload shipments. The truck has a competitive advantage over rail on the short haul because of the lower terminal cost for the truck. Although trucks do pay road taxes, they do not pay the full cost of constructing and maintaining their routes. The gap between the shipping costs of raw material and finished product has grown largely because of the higher rate charged for the truck's convenient service on finished goods. It has been the motor truck that has promoted decentralization of industry away from the old manufacturing concentrations of the Northeast. It has spread industry more evenly with population and especially helped concentrate manufacturing in large metropolitan areas.

Figure 5.2a compares the cost of truck and rail transportation. Terminal charges are greater for rail, as it takes more effort to load and put together a train than it does to load up a truck. Once moving, however, the truck costs more to operate for every mile it moves one ton of material than does rail. At some distance, say between 300 and 500 miles, the truck loses its cost advantage. However, another, and perhaps even more important, advantage is retained by the truck. That is its service superiority, one element of which is time required for delivery (Figure 5.2b). It takes considerably longer to load and put together a train of boxcars than to get a truck ready to roll. Once moving, the truck will get there faster than the railroad because of the necessity of switching boxcars and remaking trains. This delivery advantage is best summed up as convenience, and shippers are simply willing to pay higher prices for premium service.

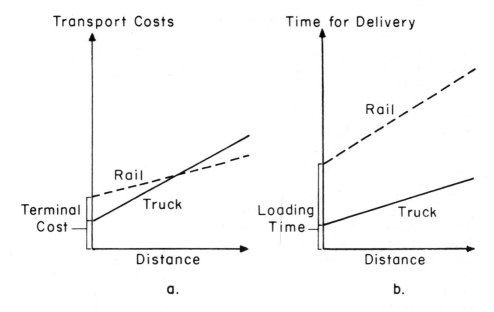

Figure 5.2a: The transport cost for rail and truck is a function of distance. However, rail has a higher terminal (handling) cost, though a lower "over-the-road" cost. The net result is that truck is most competitive in cost at shorter distances, whereas the rail is advantageous for long hauls.

Figure 5.2b: The delivery time for rail and truck is also a function of distance. Because of the slower handling speed and the generally slower movement for rail, the truck has a tremendous service advantage, even at considerable distances.

For most industry today, emphasis is on premium service rather than low cost transportation. As more manufacturing involves products with a high value per unit of weight, heterogeneous products made at a single place, and products shipped in small lots requiring door-to-door delivery, transportation service replaces transportation cost as the more significant factor in industrial location. Only those industries shipping large volumes of materials of low value per unit of weight and having simple inventory problems (homogeneous products) are still oriented to minimizing transportation costs. Such industries, so important during the earlier years of industrial growth, are a minority today, whereas industry producing high value and heterogeneous goods and requiring high quality transportation service is growing rapidly.

Quality transport service is a less confining locational influence than transportation cost. Only one or a handful of locations will permit one to achieve the lowest transport cost, but with the ubiquitous truck high quality service is possible nearly everywhere. As the role of transport cost has been declining, other influences on location have taken on greater significance. Savings possible in metropolitan locations have in general replaced savings in transportation cost as a paramount factor in the location of industry. Those cities owing their growth to past transportation advantages continue as important manufacturing centers today, though their relative significance may have decreased with the development of industry in the newer urban areas. The traditional manufacturing cities have remained important because urbanization advantages have come to replace their past transportation cost superiority.

A web of interlocking intra- and inter-industry linkages typifies metropolitan areas. A given firm is likely to require many different material supplies, each supply often needed in rather small quantities. The firm likewise may act as a supplier for a number of other industries. Where should such a firm locate to coordinate best its linkages with the several supply and demand points? The answer obviously is as near as many of them as possible, and the metropolitan area best meets this criterion. As the manufacturing process becomes more specialized and as high differentiated flows of diverse goods are shipped, an urban location becomes the most advantageous. The relative importance of intra-metropolitan movement increases relative to inter-metropolitan flow, and in this sense the largest urban areas are becoming more self-sufficient. It is, again, transportation service that is significant in the urban web of source and product linkages, not the reduction in transportation costs per se.

Increasing Role of Communication Costs

One of the most persistent economic changes in this century has been the steady growth in the "service sector." As cities have grown, a larger proportion of the labor force is employed in some service function, as opposed to agriculture and manufacturing. In part, the rise in service employment is owing to the increase in output per worker in agriculture and manufacturing, whereas there has been relatively little change by comparison in output among service workers. Rising income in general has encouraged higher per capita consumption of "luxury" goods, compared to the relative decline in consumption of foods and fibers. Both greater manufacturing and service efforts are required in the preparation and marketing of these "luxury" goods, including the creation of markets through advertising. There has been a long-term decline in the proportion of muscle power needed in our society and a corresponding increase in technical and informational skills.

In fact, brain skills have become so pervasive in almost every endeavor that the traditional categories of economic activity have begun to blur. It is now hard to tell some of the large industrialized agricultural operations from factories. These factory farms, for example, may produce milk by putting in raw materials at one end and getting out the fresh milk product at the other. The line between manufacturing and service is even more obscured, as virtually all kinds of manufacturing requires services. Is the newspaper or magazine industry in the manufacturing or service business? It is clearly in both. The old divisions would place an activity in the manufacturing category if it involved changing the form or utility of a material. Service implies the provision of information, including the transfer of confidence in selling. Today nearly all manufacturing operations rely heavily upon business services, and for a growing number of industries business services as a necessary cost item are more important than the traditional costs of transportation.

Industry has come to locate, therefore, with maximum access to needed business information services. While in the past cities that grew most rapidly were those which had sizable manufacturing employment, recent data suggests that the fastest growing urban areas are those providing the greatest service in the exchange of information. Cities, important in the past because of their locational advantages for handling materials, today are locationally desirable because they provide low cost for communication and the exchange of information.

Table 5.1 lists the thirty-three metropolitan areas in the United States with more than a million inhabitants in 1970, their percentage of population growth, and their net migration from 1960 to 1970. (Net migration is figured by substracting the number of people who moved out from the number who moved in.) Several interesting features stand out in the table. At the middle and bottom of the list, a number of "new" or previously modest sized cities appear, including Houston, Dallas, Seattle, Anaheim, Atlanta, San Diego, Miami, Denver, San Bernardino, San Jose, Tampa, and Portland. All of these cities have grown much faster than average and have had substantial net in-migration. Cities growing most sluggishly are the older ones, almost all of which are located in the old Northeastern manufacturing quarter of the nation. The Pittsburgh metropolitan area is the only city actually to lose population, with a net out-migration of 167,000 people in ten years! However, several other older industrial cities have experienced net migration losses: New York, Detroit, Cleveland, Milwaukee, Cincinnati, and Buffalo. Several cities in this list have achieved phenomenal growth through in-migration. Anaheim, virtually a Los Angeles suburb, grew more than half a million, by annexation as well as by migration. Washington, D.C., one of the busiest information handling cities, grew by over 400,000 people. Eight

Table 5.1   1970 Population Characteristics
of Metropolitan Areas in the United States
Over One Million*

S.M.S.A.	Pop. in Thousands	Rank	Percent Increase 1960-70	Net Migration in Thousands
New York	11,576		7.8	-87
Los Angeles-Long Beach	7,032	2	16.4	253
Chicago	6,979	3	12.2	10
Philadelphia	4,818	4	10.9	45
Detroit	4,200	5	11.6	-48
San Francisco-Oakland	3,110	6	17.4	183
Washington	2,861	7	38.6	417
Boston	2,754	8	6.1	N.A.
Pittsburgh	2,401	9	-0.2	-167
St. Louis	2,363	10	12.3	17
Baltimore	2,071	11	14.8	52
Cleveland	2,064	12	8.1	-45
Houston	1,985	13	40.0	310
Newark	1,857	14	9.9	10
Minneapolis-St. Paul	1,814	15	25.1	99
Dallas	1,556	16	39.1	243
Seattle-Everett	1,422	17	28.5	184
Anaheim-Santa Ana-Garden Grove	1,420	18	101.7	551
Milwaukee	1,404	19	9.8	-39
Atlanta	1,390	20	36.7	200
Cincinnati	1,385	21	9.2	-36
Paterson-Clifton-Passaic	1,359	22	14.5	64
San Diego	1,358	23	31.5	169
Buffalo	1,349	24	3.2	-84
Miami	1,268	25	35.6	254
Kansas City	1,257	26	15.0	27
Denver	1,228	27	32.2	157
San Bernardino-Riverside-Ontario	1,143	28	41.1	218
Indianapolis	1,110	29	17.6	36
San Jose	1,065	30	65.9	283
New Orleans	1,046	31	15.3	8
Tampa-St. Petersburg	1,013	32	31.2	213
Portland	1,009	33	34.9	119

*Standard Metropolitan Statistical Areas

Table 5.2   Canadian and Mexican Metropolitan
Areas over One Million Population

Canada*	Population
Montreal	2,743,208
Toronto	2,628,043
Vancouver	1,082,352
*Mexico***	
Mexico	8,541,070
Guadalajara	1,196,218
Monterrey	1,177,361

* 1971 Census data
**1970 Census data

other cities on the list gained more than 200,000 through net in-migration: Houston, San Jose, Miami, Los Angeles, Dallas, San Bernar-dino (another near suburb of Los Angeles), Tampa, and Atlanta.

Rapid metropolitan growth has not been confined only to the United States, but has been occurring in the other countries of North America, as well as elsewhere around the world. Table 5.2 presents pop-ulation data for Canadian and Mexican metropolitan areas of over one million people. Several other cities in these two countries are quickly ap-proaching the one million figure.

The conclusion is clear that we have seen major readjustments in the urban system in the past decade: exploding growth in U.S. metropolitan areas in the West and South (plus Washington, D.C.), and modest growth and relative stagnation in several industrial metropolises of the Northeast. The explanation lies largely with the advantages of the expanding cities as locations providing advanced, abundant, and inex-pensive communication and information services. Most of the fastest growing cities also have warm, pleasant climates, an attraction to those people working in informational services. Stated rather simply, advan-tages leading to past urban growth in the Northeast had to do with superior manufacturing location; advantages related to the present rapid growth of cities in the South and West stem from their specialization in services, spurring the growth of new kinds of manufacturing. For some time, expansion of manufacturing has been occurring more rapidly in the South and West than in the Northeast, though the latter still is the major area of manufacturing concentration. The spread of manufacturing away from the Northeast has been faster than the spread of population since 1929. Cities of the South and West, especially in California, specialize in information processing and consequently are points of high accessibility to detailed technical information. Put another way, places with high accessibility to particular information are locations offering low communication costs.

The Cost of Communicating

In our day-to-day activities we often do not think of communicating as bearing a cost. We go next door to visit a neighbor, bump into a friend on the street, or call someone on the telephone. And yet a cost must be assigned to the expenditure of time used in communicating, including the cost of preparing to communicate (walking to the neighbor's). Although the time-costs may not be regarded as paramount in social transactions, they may be critical in business and industrial transactions. The second kind of cost is the dollars-and-cents variety. A long distance telephone call has a charge, as does sending a letter or driving across town to visit a friend.

There are now several basic ways of communicating across long distances. Just as transportation has undergone long-term improvements, so too has the time needed to communicate between widely separated places been reduced to mere seconds. The history of communication has indeed produced a "shrinking world." By continued improvement in telephone equipment, for example, the time it takes to complete an average transcontinental call dropped from fourteen minutes in 1920 to about thirty seconds at present. Network improvements, automatic switching equipment, and direct dialing have brought New York and Los Angeles as close together as any two places in New York, for example. In dollar cost, however, there is still a difference, though the history of telephone rates has seen a general reduction in the costs of long distance communications. Before the end of this century it is likely that most households will be able to purchase a flat rate service giving unlimited access to the national telephone network. Even now Wide Area Telephone Service (WATS) gives large business and industrial users access to the national system or to specific cities at flat monthly rates. With uniform rates throughout the country, costs become independent of specific location.[3]

Postage for a letter does not depend on the distance it is sent in the country, although in the past different rates were charged by distance zones. A more significant factor is postal delivery time, in which the goal is second day delivery anywhere in the country, even though this goal is not always achieved. Highly perishable information, i.e., information which loses its significance and pertinence very quickly, is exchanged by telephone (or perhaps telegraph), whereas communication in which the time element is less critical is sent by letter.

There are other methods of information handling and exchange. Probably the most costly involves long distance travel to a point where face-to-face communication can result. Although costly, certain kinds of information can only be effectively exchanged in this way. For business and industrial personnel, travel time is far more important than the dollar cost of movement, and the many direct airline connections in large metropolitan areas are a critical consideration. Personnel travel is especially necessary for meetings in which several people are involved for the exchange of information and for decision making. Although conference telephone calls may be used for certain matters, for more complex issues and answers face-to-face and eyeball-to-eyeball meetings are necessary. Some experimental use of the visionphone (combining the telephone and television) points toward increased future reliance on this device and some possible reduction in the need for travel for face-to-face exchange. The radio, television, newspaper, magazine, and book are other means for information exchange, each with its own unique features and advantages.

The computer represents one of the greatest communication breakthroughs in man's history. It is a piece of communication equipment designed to handle information incredibly rapidly and accurately. Vast amounts of detailed information can be stored on computer cards, magnetic tapes, or magnetic disc units. A particular unit of data can be retrieved within seconds and the data manipulated (changed), added to, or deleted. The computer has meant huge cost and time savings in bookkeeping and other forms of record keeping. Its speed in retrieving information from storage and making it available on cards, printout sheets, or even in the form of graphs and maps means potential access to more information than ever before. Via telephone hookups, one does not have to be physically near his computer, as he may feed in instructions and receive back information at his remote terminal location. The time is not too distant when a large network of computers, tied via telephone hookups, will provide computing, storage, and retrieval service to users over a wide area.

Each communication device has different uses and different costs, but technology has brought about cost reductions in each case. Each of these communication systems allows the collection and accumulation of ever increasing quantities of information at one place. The location at which relevant kinds of information is collected is less critical today than ever before, but most of these "information centers" coincide with metropolitan areas. A whole new geography has been created by the speed of communicating. Areas physically remote are functionally brought close together. An industry with geographically scattered facilities becomes, in effect, functionally concentrated in terms of communication among its office headquarters, manufacturing branch plants,

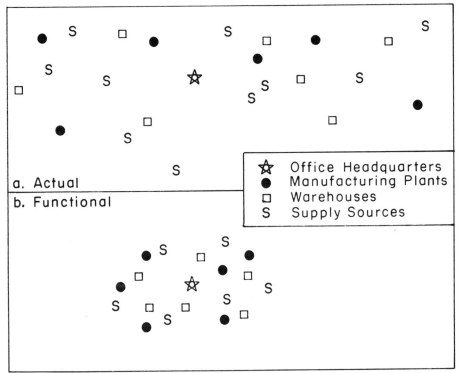

Figure 5.3a: Actual geographic locations of an office headquarters, several branch manufacturing plants, sources of materials consumed at the branch plants, and warehouses scattered over the map.

Figure 5.3b: Because of the speed and ease of communication among the scattered branch plants, material sources, warehouses, and office headquarters, the operations take on, functionally, a nearby location. Speed of communication shrinks the distances separating the various points.

warehouses, and sources of supply (Figure 5.3).

Communication linkage among the metropolitan information centers is rapid and relatively inexpensive. These major centers act as organizational points for the collection, accumulation, and processing of information. The volume of informational linkages for the larger cities depends mostly upon the relative size of the cities — not upon their distance apart, which was important in the past. Large cities have become quite tightly linked together by information flows. Smaller cities look toward larger ones for sources of information. The smaller the city, the more likely its information ties are with a larger, nearby center. And the smaller the city, the greater the likelihood that distance will play a role in the flow of information. For example, in Figure 5.4 Colorado Springs will be more strongly linked with Denver than with Kansas City, although the latter two cities are about the same size. Los Angeles and New York are closer together in communication intensity than either one is to

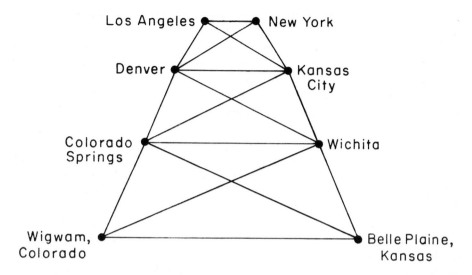

Figure 5.4: The intensity of the communication linkages among these cities is shown by the length of the connecting line, or the distance the centers are functionally apart. The larger the cities, the smaller the barrier of distance in reducing the level of communication and information flow.

Colorado Springs or to Wichita, Kansas. Further, Colorado Springs and Wichita are farther apart in communication volume than are Los Angeles and New York. In volume of telephone use, Wigwam, Colorado, 25 miles south of Colorado Springs, is "continents" away from Belle Plaine, Kansas, located a similar distance south of Wichita. These examples make for confusing geography, but they show how much communication technology has changed the map of the country.

Communication Linkages and Industry

For a modern industrial firm, it is interesting to look at information as one might a sack of flour or a ton of steel. That is, information flows into a manufacturing plant, is processed in some manner, and flows out of the plant in a different form. Just as one can assign a cost to the assembly of materials at the plant, a cost may be given to the assembly of appropriate technical, managerial, and administrative information. Information, in the form of decisions, flows out of the plants in many ways, advertising being only the best known example. Whereas it was most meaningful in the past to speak of commodity flow in manufacturing, modern industry has become so fully dependent upon accumulation, handling, and dissemination of information that a full understanding of manufacturing geography today requires the knowledge of the role of information.

Industry draws upon a diverse set of information sources. Most of these are permanently employed by the firm because of the immediate and recurring need for their services. A growing trend has been the reliance upon suppliers of business services, which specialize in providing technical information to a variety of industries. A good example is research organizations: only the very largest firms will be able to support all necessary research themselves, while other firms will draw upon research expertise from outside as the need arises. Research reports focusing upon a particular problem area are prepared by presumably objective outside sources to improve operating efficiency, product design, or packaging and shipping procedures. Tax lawyers and consultants have become increasingly important, as many decisions a firm must make today rest upon their tax impact.

Information sources relevant to manufacturing are almost entirely found in metropolitan areas. Typically, most of these services are located in the same metropolitan area in which they are consumed. They are market oriented. Even if these sources are in a different metropolis, we have seen that metropolitan areas are generally more accessible to one another than are smaller centers to metropolitan areas. In the past, accessibility within the city was so important that a central location was imperative. Today, most commonly, information oriented industries have moved to the suburbs, often where there is a cluster of similar industries.

The connection between industry and access to information is so close and strong that the geographer Pred has suggested that this connection lies at the heart of the process of urban growth.[4] Pred saw industrial growth in a city as setting into motion the foundation for urban development. New or expanded industry creates the need for expanded urban services, involving retailing, construction, and governmental activities. The expansion of urban services makes the center more attractive for new industry and spurs the expansion of existing industry. A circular causation process operates.

At the same time, the probability for industrial invention and innovation is most likely to occur in cities with considerable industrial activity. The building of a better mousetrap is most likely to be done in the mousetrap factory. Innovation and invention lead to industrial expansion and growth at the source location of the new information. Certain innovations spur the creation of entirely novel industries, which later may become dominant in the industrial composition of the metropolitan area. Henry Ford's techniques in Detroit, preceded by wagon-building in the area, resulted in localization of the automobile industry; and automobile technology made Detroit one of the largest American cities.

Once the needed information has become available to the manufacturing industry, the information must be evaluated, processed, and digested. Different kinds of information will flow by various routes — by telephone, by written word, and especially importantly by face-to-face communication. The information has not only levels of accuracy but also ranges of credibility. Generally speaking, direct interpersonal contact sorts out the issue of credibility most easily. When large amounts of tedious data need to be handled, the computer is brought into action to condense, select, or alter data. Record keeping is an important part of the computer's responsibility and of the firm's information handling.

Most information processing involves human judgments and decisions. A change in markets is anticipated. How can the manufacturing firm properly react? A competitor has found a new use for a heretofore worthless by-product. What are the implications? What course of action should be taken? A supplier of a particular item has gone out of business. What new supplier can best serve the firm's needs? A new plant has been established in Boise, Idaho. Who will manage the plant? Who will get Christmas bonuses? A million questions must be answered and must be based on solid information. Although most of these questions are not directly geographic, the point here is that the decision process operates on the basis of information, often from diverse sources, collected at one place.

An important function of the city, all too often forgotten, is its managerial role. It is the largest cities that house the headquarters and national offices for American corporations. It is here that information processing and information-based decisions are made. These cities are the nerve centers for the economy. Their tentacles snake out across the continent to make their impact felt far from the decision source. These cities are points of maximum access to information and points of maximum information output.

Likewise, at the level of the individual firm, information disseminates in a large number of ways. In fact, for all material purchased by the firm, a preceding flow of information has occurred. For shipment of manufactured goods, an information link to some destination has taken place. Every decision, no matter how routine, necessitates the movement of information from a source to a recipient. It is this information which allows the functioning of the manufacturing establishment, which ties the firm with the outside world, and which with time permits industrial changes to occur.

Previously, we noted the importance of locational cost to a manufacturing plant in terms of material, assembly, labor, product distribution, and tax cost, for example. If we add to locational cost that expense necessitated by assembling, processing, and disseminating information, a more realistic view of location will emerge. If we could somehow assign a figure to a firm's information-related costs, we would find it is a considerable percentage of the typical firm's total costs. Traditional cost categories would have to be rearranged. From the cost of a ton of steel would have to be considered the paperwork in ordering and making available that ton. Sales and advertising cost would be considered. More nebulously, the cost of decision making, including incorrect decisions, would be involved. Putting these and other factors together one would have a total information cost. Given the same firm, product line, market, etc., where should the firm locate to maximize information access at minimum communication costs?

The answer depends, of course, upon the degree to which the firm relies on information. Firms which most depend on information are characterized by some or all of the following features: (1) product modification at short notice, as is true, for example, with the style-conscious women's apparel industry; (2) sudden market shifts; (3) complex set of suppliers and/or markets; and (4) strong day-to-day competition. Although no firm will be completely indifferent to information access, some firms having a stable production schedule and operating under relatively simple manufacturing procedures will have less immediate dependence on information sources.

Figure 5.5 illustrates diagrammatically the pattern of information flows into and out of a hypothetical manufacturing firm in an urban area. The dashed lines represent information coming into the firm, the origin of each line showing geographically the information source. The type of information received includes telephone calls, letters, face-to-face conversation (with travel to the plant by consultants and travel from the plant by executives), and other means whereby information is accumulated by and for decision making at the plant. The solid lines depict the flow of information out of the plant, again by the same methods of communication. Although not shown, many of the sources of information will also be recipients because of normal two-way communication flows. The firm's geographic pattern of information movement has a definite distance effect, with the large number of local flows representing linkages within the metropolitan area. The long lines show inter-urban connections. It is clear in this fairly typical case that the firm is highly information-dependent on the local metropolis in its day-to-day operations. For any given firm, a ratio could be developed to show the proportion of these flows which begin and end within the metropolitan area compared to the proportion made outside. Such ratios would demonstrate which plants are strongly locally based in information ties and which are not. The greater the local proportion, the stronger the role of communication in the plant's location. Plants with high percentages of outside ties would seem to be less dependent on a particular metropolitan location, at least as far as communication ties are concerned.

The social communications network of the individual in the business world is related to the pattern of information flow in the firm

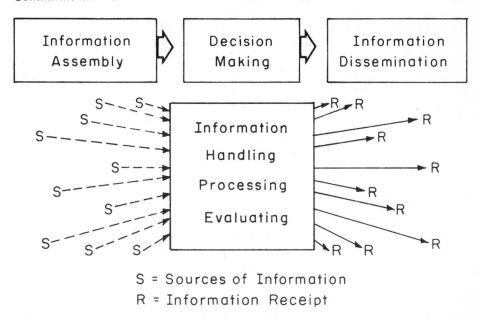

S = Sources of Information
R = Information Receipt

Figure 5.5: The flow of information into, within, and away from a manufacturing plant is analogous to the movement of material goods. Just as the greater volume of materials handled at a plant, the greater the plant's significance, so too the more information a plant processes, the greater its probability of success and significance.

which he represents. One makes social contacts within his neighborhood because the residence acts as a major reference point. The workplace is a second significant reference point. In the case of the executive and decision maker in a manufacturing enterprise, there is an overlap between the social and the business communications networks. In fact, they may be mutually reinforcing. Although many business communications remain impersonal and on a strict business basis, the very nature of information accumulation and decision making involves a social dimension. One may trust the judgment of some individuals more than others, a result of past experience in social interaction. It is very difficult actually to undertake business communication without revealing elements of one's personality, attitudes, and style — all in turn elements fundamental to social communication.

Glance back a last time to Figure 5.5. The lines not only represent information flow centering on the firm, but also the firm's business communication network. The firm's network, of course, consists of the combined networks of many individuals in the office and managerial hierarchy. Hidden from apparent view is the overlap in the firm's business network and in the sum of individual's social networks. In addition, the information handling, processing, and evaluating require a high degree of communication internal to the firm. Although once again the primary purpose of this internal communication is business, it is inevitably and at the same time woven with social coloring.

Ours is fast becoming a communication society. The large metropolitan areas are the communication centers, the storage places for information and the points of its distribution and exchange. Although even ancient cities were storehouses of information, it is through the new freedom of circulation created by technological innovation in communication that cities have come into their own and make possible the modern communication society. Urban residents are now able to become familiar with a growing body of knowledge — to such an extent that a communications overload threatens the tranquility, if not privacy, of one's life. When cities were freed from isolation by transportation improvements, large-scale manufacturing became possible. Today, as manufacturing becomes more dependent upon quick, efficient, and inexpensive communication with a growing information base, it is again the city that offers the greatest locational advantages.

Human behavior is increasingly seen as a function of the information which the individual has available to use in his decision making. Large organizations, such as manufacturing firms, are aware of the necessity to gain access to as much accurate information as possible. Owing to their great size, industrial firms organize themselves functionally and geographically to operate an efficient communication network. Whereas firms became large in the past to benefit from scale economics in the production process, today's firms gain advantage from size through communication economies. A large firm has a greater opportunity for success because it has a better communication system, both internally and with the outside world. It may also have better access to political power, as a firm's business communication network will often overlap with the political communication network.

References

1. Marvin J. Barloon, "The Interrelationship of the Changing Structure of American Transportation and Changes in Industrial Location," *Land Economics*, Vol. 41, May 1965, pp. 169 - 179.

2. Raymond Vernon, "Production and Distribution in the Large Metropolis," *Annals of the American Academy of Political and Social Sciences*, Vol. 314, 1957, pp. 15 - 29.

3. Ronald F. Abler, "Distance, Intercommunications, and Geography," *Proceedings, Association of American Geographers*, Vol. 3, 1971, pp. 1 - 4.

4. Allan R. Pred, *The Spatial Dynamics of U.S. Urban-Industrial Growth, 1800-1914* (Cambridge, Mass.: M.I.T. Press, 1966).

Chapter 6

Social Considerations in Urban Transport Policy

Urbanization has accelerated so rapidly in man's recent history, and so changed man's institutions, social and economic activities, and overall lifestyle, that new policies are required each generation, if not each decade. Transport policy is of necessity interwoven with urban policy, and urban problems need to be approached through combined urban and transport policy solutions, rather than through only one or the other. As previously noted, a basic feature of all our urban problems is the quickened pace of change. However, all too often new policy, by the time it is implemented, has become old policy and therefore an inappropriate tool with which to attack rapidly shifting problems.

Related to the use of old tools to fix new problems is the exponential growth in information. What was taught to college freshmen in Urban Planning 104 in 1960, for example, is no longer taught today, and urban planners relying on 1960 materials and approaches are ill equipped to understand and treat current planning problems. The necessity to keep abreast of any field of knowledge is rising faster than the ability of human beings to digest the expanding warehouses of knowledge. Not only do we have vast quantities of new data being analyzed, but we now have new analytic techniques and approaches for the examination of old data. Given on the one hand unprecedented change and on the other mounting and seemingly insoluble problems, Alvin Toffler in *Future Shock* explains the rise of "right-wing reversionists" who see cures coming from a heavy dose of old solutions. Likewise, "left-wing reversionists" turn to the past in offering "Marxist ideas, applicable at best to yesterday's industrialism," but clearly irrelevant to "problems of tomorrow's super-industrialism."[1]

Another approach to urban problems is to invoke the *laissez-faire* viewpoint, in which problems are thought to go away by themselves of "natural" causes just as they spontaneously arose. Human interference is seen only as an impediment to "what is meant to be," and therefore urban planning and policy are tools of the devil. What is here forgotten, of course, is that *no* policy is still *a* policy. Furthermore, the *laissez-faire* solution ignores the point that decision making on the individual, family, and group levels continually operates in urban areas and is the collective cause of our urban problems. Their cure should lie in policy decisions that smooth out and minimize the conflicting aspirations of individuals and groups by anticipating future change. In transport policy, conflicts are especially common because the anticipated benefits at one location often make for dreaded consequences at another place.

In beginning to understand transport policy, it is fruitful to think of transportation as linking together the three sectors of the economy, primary production (relying largely upon natural resources), secondary production (manufacturing), and tertiary activity (making available goods and services). A change in transport policy may affect any one of these sectors. For example, agriculture in a particular area may be encouraged by a decision to improve road connections with a market area. Or a small retail establishment may be forced out of business by a new road permitting customers to travel to a large integrated shopping center. The economic sectors have an impact on transport decisions as well; for example, a policy to reduce cotton acreage may reduce freight hauls in some areas but increase hauls in places more favored for cotton production. A policy to disperse industry for strategic reasons also has a differential impact upon the transportation system. Therefore, transport policy cannot be created in isolation.

This realization, when it has been realized at all, has often led to the employment of cost-benefit analysis. The expected costs of a new highway, for example, are weighed against its anticipated benefits. On the cost side, fairly accurate forecasts may be made, since material, labor, and right-of-way costs are usually known. In the past, these costs have frequently been estimated too low, however, because of the general rise in costs from the time of estimate to the time of project completion. The economic benefits are somewhat more difficult to measure precisely, but nevertheless dollars-and-cents values can be given which can be directly compared to costs. Although economic costs and benefits may be compared in the same measurement unit, the social costs and benefits can hardly be measured at all, and an attempt to give them dollars-and-cents meaning is largely guesswork.

What are the social costs or benefits of family relocations from the path of a freeway? What are the social costs of automobile accidents and deaths? What are the social benefits of increases in mobility? The difficulty in answering such questions is seen in the inability to grasp the proper trade-offs between social costs and benefits. How many automobile deaths must be run up before the advantages of an increase in travel mobility become a net social loss? Here precise mathematical functions become anyone's vague guess. We need to be able to say that in achieving one unit of mobility we will bring about a reduction of X units in neighborhood stability. But how does one compare apples and pumpkins? How do we begin measuring all these varied elements in common units?

And this is only half of the problem. Once social liabilities and assets are known, how should these be weighed against the economic costs and benefits? When economic advantages are associated with social disadvantages, what policies exist to resolve such dilemmas? Typically, the problem is complicated by the fact that advantages and disadvantages fall unequally upon different groups and different locations. What is a highway benefit to one group is a disaster to another.

Clearly policies are required to sort out the salient issues. Even though we may not be able to arrive at a mathematically precise agreement on costs and benefits in transportation decisions, at least we may endeavor to grapple with the issues in a fair and enlightened manner. We must recognize that in any transport decision there are non-transport implications for the society and the economy, just as major societal and economic changes reverberate in the transport system. The benefits and the damage are unevenly distributed, geographically and demographically. Policy must trade off current assets and liabilities with anticipated future assets and liabilities.

Transportation Policy and the City

One overall objective of a transport policy is to minimize the undesirable and to maximize the desirable consequences. Construction cost is one unavoidable feature of creating a new highway, and it is a cost to be reduced as much as possible for a given quality of roadway. Increased opportunity for mobility is deemed a positive aspect of highway development. Presumably, a greater number of destinations can be reached, more rapid travel times are possible, and the cost of movement is lowered.

The economic and social costs of an urban transport facility are not evenly spread geographically, but tend to be localized. Figure 6.1 shows the hypothetical economic costs and benefits of an urban highway, assuming an equally spread population, income level, taxation system, and mobility preference. The vertical axis is the economic costs and

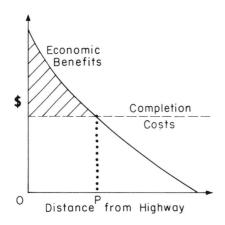

Figure 6.1: When completion costs of a highway are spread evenly over the urban population, the majority of the economic benefits go to those living near the highway; up to distance P economic benefits exceed costs.

benefits; the horizontal axis measures distance away from the highway (located at zero distance). Assuming taxation is levied equally on all people, the cost of construction is borne evenly geographically. However, those living nearest the new highway will reap the highest economic benefits, as they will be located to take maximum advantage of the services offered. With growing distance away from the highway, the economic benefits will begin to taper off. There is, under these assumptions, a given distance, *P*, at which the per capita economic benefits exactly match the construction cost for that point. Up to that distance, therefore, economic costs are lower than benefits; beyond that distance they are higher. A basic policy issue emerges from this illustration: How far should the tax base reach beyond the area of significant economic benefits?

Social costs and benefits have a different geographic pattern with reference to distance away from an urban highway. In Figure 6.2 per capita social costs are shown more immediately confined to a small impact area paralleling the highway on either side. These are the costs of neighborhood disruption and family relocation, as well as the temporary problem of construction noise and inconvenience. Social benefits, by their very nature, are diffused throughout society, but they nevertheless demonstrate some geographic concentration near the highway. For example, the increased mobility made possible by the highway gives the highway user access to a wider information base within the city and allows the opportunity for, though does not guarantee, a higher quality life within the social system.

A distinction should be made between so-called user and non-user benefits. The former refer to advantages realized by those who actually utilize the transport facility. Non-user benefits go to the community or society in general and to specific economic activities, such as service stations, motels, and restaurants. Immediate impact is felt by those who

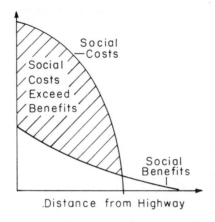

.Distance from Highway

Figure 6.2: Whereas social benefits of a new highway decline slowly away from the highway, the social costs (relocation and disruption) are strongly felt in the immediate area of the construction.

use a transport service, but non-user consequences are by nature longer term in their effect. Figure 6.3 compares the intensity of a highway's impact over time for automobile drivers who may select the new route and for activities located along the route. As soon as the highway is opened, traffic pours onto the concrete anticipating the benefits of increased mobility. The impact on activities located along the highway may be barely noticeable initially. At first, highway oriented retail outlets (service stations, motels, and restaurants) will note an increase in business. Next new highway oriented activities may be built to compete with existing retail establishments. Certain highways will attract strip development, such as "hamburger row" or "automobile row." Non-user impact is now felt.

Over an even longer period of time, the highway may be one of a series of attractive features encouraging the location of new industry utilizing truck transportation. Industry draws in labor, enlarging the population base of the city. As the city grows, new and larger retail establishments are needed. A circular causation model has been set into mo-

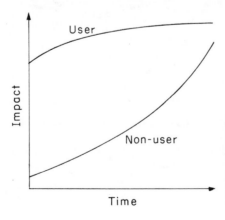

Time

Figure 6.3: When a new highway is put into service, the impact is at first most strongly felt by the highway user, though the impact will increase only slowly with time. For the non-user impact will also be felt in changing land uses near the highway, but these changes become greater over time.

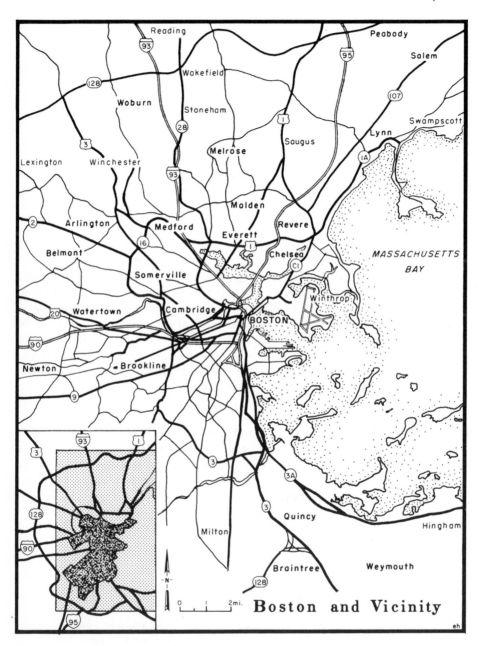

Figure 6.4:   The configuration of streets and highways in Boston, an "old" city. The layout is geometrically irregular, with a focus on downtown.

tion, one link in the chain being the highway. The highway cannot by itself insure a positive impact for adjacent activities, but given a sufficient length of time these benefits will normally grow. However, as time passes these benefits become more and more difficult to attribute directly to the highway.

Although social impact may derive from the direct use of the highway, its accumulated and indirect impact is most commonly in the non-user category. A good way to look at the indirect social effect is by asking the questions: What would the social space of our cities be like under a different transportation regime? How would a different transportation system have affected the land use arrangements and living space in the city?

For an answer, let us turn to the street and highway systems of Boston, an old city which grew up in the pre-automobile era, and Los Angeles, which achieved its greatest growth with the machine. Although the car has superimposed its effect on historic Boston, the old street pattern has guided the new freeway layout. In Figure 6.4, the routes focus on downtown Boston. The older streets angle their way towards the city's heart. Street junctions are only by chance at right angles. The Charles and Mystic Rivers guide the street pattern, except where traffic energy builds up to demand a bridge crossing. The bevy of surrounding suburbs are linked rather directly with central Boston. The freeway system follows the same directional focus on downtown Boston, as routes pour in from all directions (except Massachusetts Bay to the east). In addition, a perimeter belt (Route 128) ties together the outer suburbs, and farther out I-495 directs traffic around the congested metropolitan area.

Figure 6.5 represents a striking contrast. The street and highway pattern of the Los Angeles area is regular and geometric compared to Boston's. Most streets meet at right angles, and even the interstate layout displays a large measure of regularity. Basically lacking is a single focus for the diffused route pattern. Los Angeles and its numerous suburbs truly represent a multi-centered metropolis.

Although the Boston and Los Angeles contrasts do not stem from conscious and directed differences in transport policy, they do reflect an example of differences that have emerged from different transport experiences. Furthermore, they point up the basic role transport plays in the physical layout and arrangement of the city. In Los Angeles, population density is lower and spread more widely, and commercial and industrial activities are everywhere diffused. Social values and attitudes are scrambled by the luxury of increased mobility bringing together people of disparate age, background, and geography. The social space of these two cities is cut up differently by the geometry of streets and highways.

Los Angeles, as everyone knows, is a city of freeways — some say

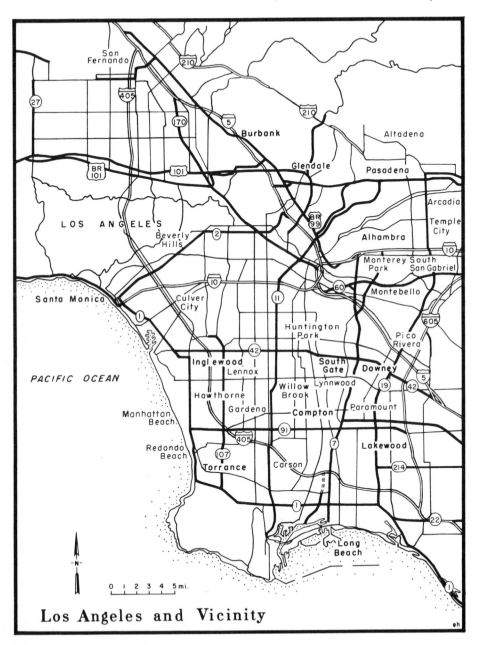

Figure 6.5: The configuration of streets and highways in Los Angeles. The layout is basically at right angles, with many foci.

a freeway with cities. Clearly it represents one policy alternative which urban transportation may take — the urban freeway and the automobile society. The most obvious policy alternative is a city featuring transit or a combination of automobiles and transit hookups at strategic points having large parking facilities. How do these alternatives stack up in economic and social terms?

As previously noted, metropolitan transportation problems basically occur during peak hours, when traffic densities exceed highway capacities. The largest share of this congestion must be put on the downtown commuter. Highway financing relies on user charges based essentially on the same rate per vehicle mile in all parts of the urban area. And yet economic and social costs of mobility vary significantly geographically. Specifically, making available high capacity transport facilities for workers in the central part of the city is extremely expensive. It follows that the downtown commuter may not be paying his share for the transport service he uses and is in effect subsidized by others in the metropolitan area. Provision of this expensive service benefits a particular group of suburban dwellers whose skin and collars are generally white.

The social cost of a freeway running downtown is also unequally felt geographically. As the freeway is placed through the more lightly populated suburbs, open space for its path can fairly readily be found, and the adjacent population and land use is only nominally affected. That same freeway, however, as it heads downtown runs into increasingly valuable and expensive land. It also cuts into heavily populated areas, displacing people, jobs, and shopping facilities. In the case of the downtown freeway, the immediate social upheaval is felt most acutely by those who are in fact economically subsidizing the suburban user to race through his community (or ex-community) to a downtown destination. The central city resident, while being raped by freeway penetration, is forced to pay for a service he cannot equally enjoy.

The circumferential freeway has a different set of geographically spread benefits and disbenefits. The circumferential is intended to divert traffic from the congested core and route it around the city. To the extent that the freeway is used by intercity travelers, the city users may subsidize those merely passing through. On the other hand, avoidance of increased congestion is a social benefit to all concerned. For local residents, use of the circumferential may bring about considerable travel savings and permit access to otherwise remote locations around the city. Most frequent users of the belt highway are those who live within its easy travel reach, those who presumably bear whatever social dislocation is associated with its immediate construction.

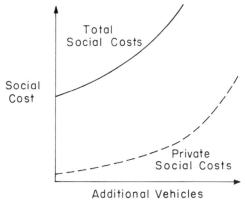

Additional Vehicles

Figure 6.6: Highway congestion results in the frustrating social cost of delay; yet the private or individual social costs are only a small fraction of total social costs.

Now it would seem reasonable that a transportation policy should be rooted in cost considerations, both economic and social. The costs of transit, either rail or express bus, are lower per person trip than for automobile. Many estimates claim automobile travel is two to four times as expensive as transit. The economist will tell us that when a commodity is in short supply its price will rise until supply is equal to demand. Cannot one, therefore, place higher charges on the heaviest users of scarce services? Should not some taxation scheme be implemented to charge those wishing to make use of urban roads during rush hours when transport services are in shortest supply? A higher charge would discourage use and reduce congestion.

This solution has not proven very helpful, since overall congestion at the present time could be reduced by use of cheap transit. There are several other reasons. First, the automobile user does not consider the full cost of operating his vehicle on a single trip; he thinks only — if at all — of his out-of-pocket costs for gasoline. Secondly, there is a tenacious consumer preference for the automobile, with its privacy and flexibility, even with the certainty of traffic delays. Thirdly, a huge public outcry would greet sharply increased costs of automobile operation during peak hours, to say nothing of the problem of implementing and maintaining such a system. Finally, only very large rises in the cost differential between auto and transit would encourage a significant switch to transit use.

A fundamental problem with the congestion induced by the automobile is its social cost. The social cost of delay may be spread over a stream of traffic by the addition of one vehicle. The driver is not discouraged from pulling into a traffic stream by the small fraction of the total congestion he must contend with. Even though he has added, say, ten units to the total social cost by his presence on the highway, he will "consume," say, only one unit of that social cost. Figure 6.6 shows the relationship between the social cost of delay (including driving frustra-

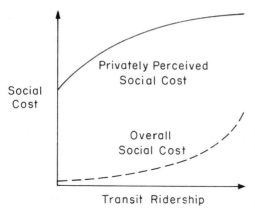

Social Cost

Privately Perceived
Social Cost

Overall
Social Cost

Transit Ridership

Figure 6.7: For transit, increased ridership brings about an overall reduction in the social cost of delay, but the privately or individually perceived social cost of transit use is extremely high.

tion) and the addition of vehicles to a given road facility. As the first several vehicles are added, the social costs rise rather slowly until a noticeable level of congestion is reached, whereupon social cost climbs more sharply. A similar curve of social cost is experienced by the individual driver, except that he is bearing only a tiny proportion of the overall costs. When there is a mild level of congestion, the proportion of total cost falling on any one motorist is higher than during severe congestion, but the intensity of social disbenefits is greater to him during the latter situation.

With transit, surprisingly, a different relationship between social cost and ridership numbers exists. Here the individual social costs are perceived to be greater than the total social cost. The sum of the parts exceeds the total! Examine Figure 6.7. The overall social cost of increasing transit usage rises rather slowly because of the space-economical features of transit and the resulting lack of congestion. In fact, for bus transit most congestion is created by competition from automobiles. However, the perceived private social cost to an individual goes up very suddenly with increased ridership. Here it is not delay so much that enters the social cost as it is the intrusion of strangers on one's privacy and personal social space. Some delays, nevertheless, may result in making connections or waiting for transit service. As ridership increases, crowding becomes a greater problem and the annoyances and frustrations of mass-packaging human beings become increasingly intolerable.

Urban Policy and Transportation

The millions of people living in cities in the United States participate daily in creating the cities of tomorrow. A host of private citizens with their own personal aspirations, needs, and perceptions make decisions about the use of urban land. Although guided by certain

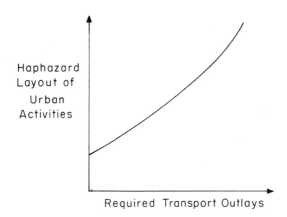

Haphazard
Layout of
Urban
Activities

Required Transport Outlays

Figure 6.8: The more haphazard the arrangement of urban land uses, the more investment is needed in transportation in order to link the inefficient pattern of land use together.

economic, social, and geographic principles — often only dimly recognized — these individual locational decisions are made without guidance from comprehensive urban planning goals. The result is a badly jumbled city, where activities and people are not efficiently located for ease of functioning. The city strives to make the scrambled pattern of land use more effective and efficient by improving transportation and other city services. But as Figure 6.8 shows, the more crazy-quilt the distribution of urban activities, the higher the transportation cost required to cope with making the city work. In most cities advanced transportation technology is propping up all manner of inefficiencies in a barely tolerable urban environment.

Attempting to create a transportation policy in isolation from the reality of urban space is at best a patch-up policy. It is fiddling with the holes in the dike while the water rises. It is applying a few exterior Band-Aids while the patient internally bleeds to death. Instead of a short-sighted fix-it approach, what is desperately needed is urban policy in a truly comprehensive sense. Such a policy must be future oriented and must have as its goal community design that makes the urban surroundings work effectively for human beings. Because of the reciprocal relationships between urban land use and transportation, any urban policy must integrate transportation as a fundamental component of the overall development strategy. Future urban goals should be not merely to alleviate problems of living in cities but to create a new style of urban environment in which problems are minimized in the first place. A large dose of optimism is a much needed initial step toward planning and building toward the future.

At the present time a pervading pessimism prevails among Americans regarding the future of our cities, and it is easy to see why. Slums; traffic congestion and accidents; juvenile and other crimes; unemployment; water, air, and noise pollution; crowding in schools; racial segregation and related minority problems; and costs of urban government are all growing, while at the same time there is a reduction of play space, of social responsibility, and of urban amenities. This unpleasant urban environment has been created at a considerable capital investment over a long period of time, and despite its repellant appearance and disordered functioning there are many who seem to believe that significant improvement would simply cost too much money. They argue that there is too much capital sunk into and intertwined with our present problems to make restoration more than a utopian dream.

And yet if we look back a few decades, we see a nation whose cities by present standards were of reasonably modest size, whose problems, though they existed, were not of today's ugly dimensions, and most importantly whose future expansion was to be extensive. Although that growth was not well planned, the lesson for today should be clear. Cities are continuing to grow. All future predictions place tens of millions of additional people in our cities by the year 2000, with the area devoted to cities expected to double. Surely some planning guideposts need to be erected for building construction and the location of urban retailing, industry, and services. Although a great opportunity for planning was missed in the past, a greater challenge to plan confronts us now, as we must not only create new living space but make old urban space livable.

We are paying a high social cost for past omissions. Transportation is called upon to make our old cities work in a modern era. As transportation struggles to overcome space, urban space threatens to overcome transportation. We splice our cities together with transport arteries to compensate for lack of comprehensive urban planning, and the resulting transportation system itself lacks any plan. Furthermore, the planless transport system creates its own land use arrangements, themselves unplanned for and uncoordinated. The extent to which transportation has helped destroy the city, however, is an indication of its potential to renovate urban areas and to guide future city expansion.

A coordinated urban and transportation policy is needed, probably at the Federal level, since urban problems are national problems repeated in virtually every urban area. Despite this need for a single comprehensive plan, we are confronted by a bewildering array of bits and pieces of policy, some directly and others indirectly involving the city and its transportation system. The Federal-Aid Highway Act of 1956 setting up the National System of Interstate and Defense Highways has been one example of a policy that has had unforeseen and manifold consequences for cities. Established as a grandiose plan to link major urban centers of the country, the interstate was also built through and around these cities, and has encouraged the alarming spread of cities into the countryside. Although we may be able to cross the continent without a traffic light, we cannot get through the clogged city without coming to a dead halt.

At the same time that dispersal of the city is encouraged by one policy, another works toward the concentration of activities in the old ci-ty. Urban renewal has bombed the central city, ridding it of some of its slums but not of its poor people. Urban renewal programs have at-tempted to remedy the physical deterioration and blight of the innercity, and make the downtown as viable as in the days before widespread suburbanization. However, urban blight and decay are not the causes but the consequences of the urban slum system, and renewal has attacked the manifestation, not the cause of deterioration. The people living in formerly blighted neighborhoods were not renewed in job training, education, or level of urban living. They made way for the civic and cultural facilities, the expansion of educational institutions, industrial sites, and shopping plazas. A new set of activities was established to rebuild and strengthen the downtown. A painful dislocation and up-heaval of thousands upon thousands of families took place, which led to increased population densities at other low-income housing locations. Urban renewal, with its objective of revitalizing the downtown, has been able to achieve this goal only at a social cost that is more and more recognized as being prohibitively high.

Urban renewal policy makes assumptions about the nature of the housing market. While it recognizes the need to replace low-income housing in a deteriorating condition, it at the same time assumes that a vacancy exists in low-income housing sufficient to absorb the displaced families. A major use of renewed areas is for high-income rental units (high-rise apartments). A second assumption therefore is that there exists a proper level of demand for high rent apartment units, meaning that a shortage of high-income housing must exist. In most cities most of the time there is a shortage of low-income shelter and a surplus of high-income housing. Urban renewal, at best, seems to be a policy to en-courage slum migration from one part of the innercity to another, accom-panied by a high proportion of vacancies in the high-rise apartments that have replaced former slums.

Juxtaposed with the policy of building high-income housing in the innercity is highway policy encouraging upper-income households to locate their residences away from the innercity. In addition, the Federal policy facilitating home loans for middle- and upper-income families favors suburban location. Two sets of policies are working at opposite ends, without full realization of what the policies have led to.

Many other examples could be cited of urban policies which con-flict with one another in stated objectives and which impose diametrically different demands on the transportation system. One of the most fun-damental reasons for conflicting policies is the multiplicity of political units in the typical metropolitan area. In the early 1960s there were over 18,000 governmental units in just over 200 standard metropolitan statistical areas, and the number of units has continued to grow during the past decade. Each unit has its own separate priorities, policies, and plans. The vested interests of local governments are too powerful to expect the creation of many metropolitan governments of the type in Dade County, Florida; Davidson County, Tennessee; Toronto, Canada; and in several other metropolitan areas in the Province of Ontario.

Nevertheless, comprehensive planning is on the upsurge. The Federal Highway Act of 1962 required that by mid-1965 spending on metropolitan highways be preceded by comprehensive transportation planning. Initially many cities were poorly prepared to provide such planning. The steps of data collection, analysis, and projection to future patterns were all too often blurred by temporal constraints. After spending several months conducting interviews and carrying out mapping exercises, one group of planners found the deadline fast approaching by which their comprehensive plan was to be completed. Housed in one room was a formidable stack of IBM cards containing the collected data, now ready for analysis. In the adjacent room worked a small group of planners, perspiring heavily as they hurriedly wrote out plans based on their own benign intuition. Their deadline was met, a plan had been created, but that plan had nothing to do with the data collection stage. No time had been given to the analysis of this data, from which the plan was supposed to have evolved. Fortunately, such practices happen less frequently today, and plans are formulated after careful analysis of existing conditions linked to visions of what future urban living could be like.

If the results of past policy did not exactly square with quality of living considerations, it was only because planners felt unable to start with a clean slate. Future change was too strongly locked in with past problems. However, quality of life cannot always be measured with money, for life is governed by feelings, attitudes, and perceptions.

The field of transportation has grown up with a strong economic bias. Many of the great classical economists in the early part of this century were concerned with transport economics. Today a large literature exists in this field, with a whole shelf of introductory textbooks describing the economics of transportation. Next to it stands a nearly empty shelf devoted to social aspects of transportation. It is toward the empty shelf that the planner is reaching to find out how to incorporate quality of living in his transportation plans. Environmental quality is one important facet of living, but by no means the only one. We need to learn more about the impact of society on our transportation system and the effect of our transportation on society.

References

1. Alvin Toffler, *Future Shock* (New York: Bantam Books, 1970), p. 361.

Chapter 7

Circulation, Planning, and the Future Urban Society

This chapter seeks to do three things. As a foundation and backdrop, it discusses the process of urban transportation planning and the problems of implementing the best laid plans. Secondly, this chapter points up the enormously critical and pervasive roles cities will play in the future as they spread ever farther over the landscape. Finally, tying planning with future cities, some prescriptions are offered for planning and public policy relating to transportation and communications in our urban future.

Urban Transportation Planning

It is instructive to review the transportation planning process as it has evolved over the past quarter century. At the present time, the steps in urban transportation planning are much the same in all urban areas engaged in planning, and differences have to do primarily with the varying amount of time and money spent on each particular step. The transportation planning process results in a study or report setting down plans for new transportation facilities or for modifying old ones. Logically, these plans have a locational component that shows the geographical distribution of forecasted facilities.

Transportation planning studies are carried out by teams of professionals, typically from a great variety of academic disciplines.[1] In this way, experience and training from many points of view can be brought to bear on a particular planning problem. The largest

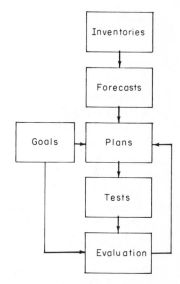

Figure 7.1: The necessary steps in the transportation planning process. Source: From Roger L. Creighton, *Urban Transportation Planning* (Urbana: University of Illinois Press), p. 136.

metropolitan areas usually have their own established planning teams which spend several years in arriving at the final planning document. Smaller cities may contract with a professional, private planning group that carries out studies for numerous cities. In either case, large financial outlays are necessary, whether from municipal or state highway funds, or from the Bureau of Public Roads or other federal agencies.

The initial step in the normal planning process is to undertake an inventory of existing facilities (transportation and land use) and the utilization of these facilities (Figure 7.1). This step includes mapping land uses, population and employment densities, and surveying origins and destinations for various types of trips, traffic counts on streets, and perhaps parking facilities. Data is collected by household interview, and normally socioeconomic and demographic characteristics of the household are also included. The data is then coded numerically for computer storage, manipulation, and analysis.

Based on the inventoried data, forecasts are then made to depict the city at some future time period; they involve a variety of assumptions and therefore all the hazards that one might expect from attempting to peer into the future. These forecasts try to show future distributions of people, employment, and shopping, and to project needed transportation facilities based on the anticipated distributions. Alternative forecasts derived from different assumptions may be made.

Perhaps the most difficult and yet most critical step in the entire planning process is setting down the goals, since any plan must be judged in terms of whether or not it meets its stated objectives. Goals are basically subjectively determined, even though some of them may be measured and quantified. The objectives must be realistic and consistent with one another. Although some trade-off between objectives is possible, diametrically opposed objectives will only cloud the already complex planning process. It is here in the realm of goals or objectives that planning most often falls down. All too frequently, trite or platitudinous goals are thrust forward to take the place of precisely worded and carefully thought out objectives.

From the interplay between forecasts and goals, specific transportation plans are derived. These plans indicate the transportation facilities needed by a particular year, based on projected population distribution and economic activities. The plans must obviously take into consideration a great many factors and be comprehensive in terms of the impact on the entire urban system. Specific types of materials are typically assembled in drawing up plans, such as air photos, large-scale maps, and previous plans, if any. Generation of the plans calls for inputs from transportation engineering and traffic flow theory. Calculations need to be made to determine the volume and spacing of vehicles over existing and planned streets, for example. The goals of the planning process must of course be closely integrated with the development of the plan.

Once transportation plans are drawn up, it is necessary to test how well these plans will work. One testing method, all too often used in the past, is simply to wait twenty years and find out. Unfortunately, this method has frequently revealed weaknesses in the plans, but by then it is clearly too late to effect a remedy, since money has already been sunk into an inefficient and unsatisfactory transportation system. It is now possible, however, to test the result of a plan by use of computer simulation models. These models incorporate numerous "rules," or constraints, describing how reality is thought to operate. Real world data is used as input, along with forecasts to project the data into a future time frame. This testing of the transportation plan, or plans, is meant to detail how satisfactory the proposed transportation system is likely to be in terms of moving traffic, connecting different parts of the urban area with transport facilities, reducing congestion on links in the transportation system, and generally solving the transportation problems facing the urban area.

The last step in the planning process, prior to implementation, is evaluation of the plans based on comparing the results of simulation testing with the goals previously set. The goals are matched against the plan itself or, frequently, different plans in order to select the most beneficial plan. The purpose of evaluation is to select the best plan and to improve the plan — thus the feedback loop from evaluation to plans in Figure 7.1.

Once these several steps have been accomplished, a written plan, along with diagrams, maps, and other supporting documentation, is public. Usually, those who have participated in drawing up the urban transportation plan are not those who decide whether or not the plan will be implemented. Although costs of various proposals will be stated in the plans, the availability and allocation of funds will be the concern of a different segment of the metropolitan governmental system. In fact, the plans may call for cooperation among various municipal governments within the metropolitan area, and disagreement by even one of these municipal units may be sufficient to block the best designed plan. What is actually done with plans may bear little connection to the quality of those plans, as political considerations lie between the planning process and implementation.

A specific example will suffice in which plans could not be placed into operation, in this case not because of governmental intervention but because of the role of private individuals. This scenario illustrates one of the most central issues involving planning in a society which has long advanced the role of the individual. It addresses the conflict between the "good of society," individual rights, and the profit motive.

Figure 7.2 illustrates a small portion of a larger plan for transportation and land use in a peripheral section of a major metropolitan area. The scale here is the '"neighborhood," defined on two sides by major traffic arteries. Occupying the corner location is to be a small neighborhood shopping center, abutted on one side by high-rise apartments and on another by an office complex designed as a buffer between the commercially zoned land and a residential area. The proposed residential land use includes town house apartments and high, medium, and low density single family dwellings. Near the center is a school and a large park. The plan is well designed in that it integrates transportation requirements with land use. Land uses generating the heaviest traffic lie near the major arteries, with lower density uses located on less traveled residential streets. Some environmental considerations have been recognized in the plan, as the stream flowing through the area is used, in part, as a buffer between different kinds of residential areas.

Implementation of this plan had to await commercial and real estate developers who were expected to operate within the local zoning regulations as indicated by the plan. However, before any development had taken place a large national corporation became interested in a plot of this land for establishing a branch plant. Since the plant would manufacture decorative glassware, employ relatively few workers, and add significantly to the tax base of the suburban municipality in which it would locate, ways were sought to alter the zoning regulations to accommodate it. The industry was permitted to locate in the area which had previously been designated for tower apartments, and it was generally agreed that no serious violation of the original plan had taken place at this time.

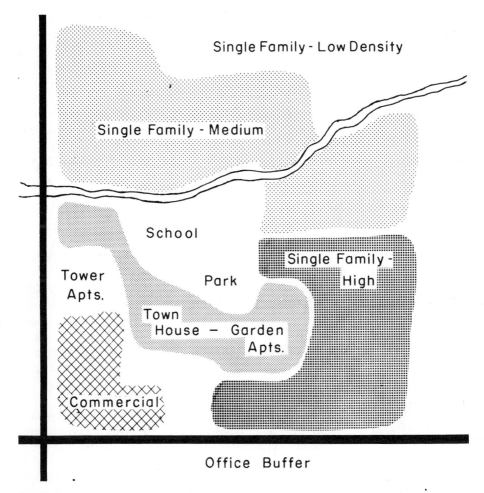

Figure 7.2: An example of a well-planned neighborhood, illustrating a part of a larger metropolitan transportation and land use plan.

Shortly thereafter, a second industrial firm became interested in a location adjacent to the glassware firm and next to the stream. This firm was to manufacture garden tractor pistons. The water site was important because of the firm's need to extract a small amount of water for cooling machinery. Virtually all of the water would be returned to the stream at only a slightly higher temperature. Although this firm would employ more workers and be less compatible with the proposed residential developments, again the tax revenue would be significant, and if the firm were refused a zoning change it would simply locate elsewhere to another community's tax benefit. Already, serious damage to the original plan was occurring.

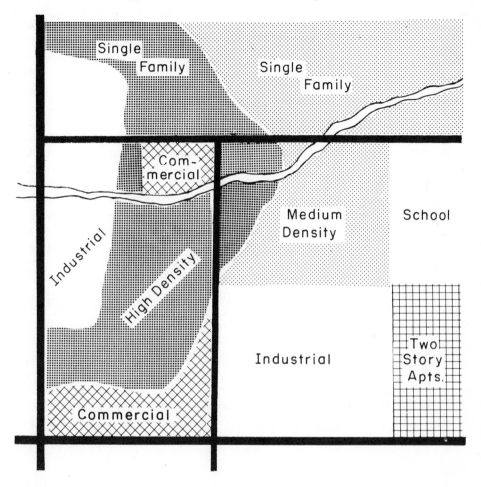

Figure 7.3: An example of the land use and transportation pattern that actually developed in an area which had a good plan that was not followed in the development process.

It then became clear that the school-park complex would have to be relocated. A real estate developer proposed encircling the two industries with high density single family dwellings, each lot being extremely small and each house selling for a modest price within the reach of workers in the piston plant, which was already expanding its plant operations to the north of the stream. By this time the original plan was virtually abandoned, and zoning changes were easily made.

Over the next decade, a land use and transportation pattern had evolved in this area bearing almost no resemblance to the area's original plan. Figure 7.3 shows the results of this unguided development. First of all, instead of two major traffic arteries, there are now four heavily traveled routes with four congested intersections; and segments of these arteries cut through residential areas. The school is less centrally located, the park has not materialized, and the commercial development is fragmented. The resulting land use and transportation pattern was almost completely unplanned, despite the existence of a very good plan before any development had occurred.

This illustration has been repeated many times over in a large number of metropolitan areas.[2] Yet it demonstrates only one kind of impediment to carrying out well designed and carefully thought out plans. The several steps in the transportation planning process, from traffic and land use inventories and forecasting to testing and evaluating plans tied to specific goals, had not contributed positively to the resulting pattern of land use, traffic flow, and transportation facilities in the example above.

Cities will certainly continue to change. Up to now, urban growth and change has come about by the interaction of a complex set of economic, social, and political forces operating on their own without any significant planned influence. The role of transportation and communications has been central to generating this unplanned urban change, if only because of the two-way cause and effect between circulation and land use. The planning sciences are in their relative infancy at the present time, on the one hand still experimenting with their planning methodology and models and on the other operating on a day-to-day basis under a fairly rigid and mechanical set of procedures. What then will our future cities be like, what role will planning come to occupy in their change, and what manner of circulation within and among them will be prominent in bringing about this new generation of cities?

The Spread of Future Cities

In a geographic sense, clustered human settlement has gone through three stages or generations. The first was the isolated community of campsite, village, town, or small city, confined spatially and entirely local in orientation. Planning was of little concern when living and working space was small and when densities of people and activities were low. A second stage in human settlement might be designated the true city, an urban area in which a significantly larger population turned to city living and in which the city expanded its influence over an extensive territory, region, or country. In this stage the urban area remained physically isolated from other urban settlements, although its population and activities spread far into the surrounding countryside. It was at this stage that the need for planning became mandatory, as the city had grown so complex and had so many independent decision makers in inherent conflict. The result was the jumbled, troubled city with which we are so

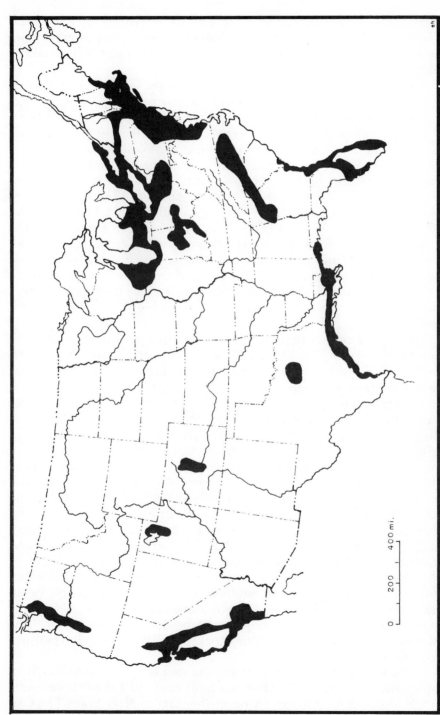

Figure 7.4: Emerging Megalopolises or continuous urbanized areas spreading across the U.S. landscape.

familiar today in North America, as well as elsewhere in the world. However, the third generation of city development promises even more complexity and further challenges our planning vision and policy making capabilities.

In the late 1950s and early 1960s Jean Gottmann, a French geographer, recognized the emergence of a new process of urbanization occurring on the eastern seaboard of the United States.[3] He mapped and analyzed a continuous stretch of urban and suburban areas extending some 600 miles from north of Boston to south of Washington, D.C. This chain of metropolitan areas was rapidly growing together to create a supermetropolitan form, a continuous city which he termed "Megalopolis," the third stage in human settlement. The great historic cities of the east coast — Boston, New York, Philadelphia, Baltimore, and Washington — grew because of their location between Europe and the U.S. interior, and assumed a position of dominance in economic, political, financial, cultural, and manufacturing affairs. The dominance of these cities led to their outward growth, the development of extensive suburbs, and the functional dependence of satellite centers. The metropolitan areas coalesced to form the continuously urbanized Northeastern seaboard, Megalopolis.

The 1970 census shows the trend toward megalopolitanization to be accelerating and to be characteristic of more and more parts of the United States.[4] Figure 7.4 maps areas in the most advanced stages of becoming megalopolises, areas which will be almost entirely urbanized in the next ten, twenty, or thirty years. Look first at the east coast. Connecting with the seaboard megalopolis described by Gottmann is an arm extending up the Hudson River in New York state to Albany, where an abrupt turn to the west carries the emerging megalopolis along the Mohawk Gap (through Schenectady, Utica, Syracuse, Rochester, to Buffalo). Only a thin finger extends southward along Lake Erie to link the New York Megalopolis with the Pittsburgh-Cleveland Megalopolis. Around the southern and western end of Lake Erie is a connector with the Detroit-Southern Michigan Megalopolis. With Detroit at its core, this urbanized area extends northward through Flint to Saginaw-Bay City and westward to Lake Michigan to encompass Ann Arbor, Jackson, Lansing, Battle Creek, Kalamazoo, and Grand Rapids. The Lake Michigan Megalopolis wraps around the southern end of the lake (South Bend, Elkhart, and Gary, Indiana) and north along the west side of the lake through Chicago and its numerous suburbs and satellites to north of Milwaukee, bulging westward to Rockford, Illinois, and Madison, Wisconsin.

In Canada, the Detroit metropolitan area spills over into Windsor, Ontario, and from there an urbanized path north of Lake Erie connects with the Mohawk Gap urban string in the state of New York. The Ontario Megalopolis swings around the western end of Lake Ontario, where it is now centered on the city of Hamilton, and extends as far west as Kitchener. North of Lake Ontario, the urbanized area is anchored by Toronto on the west and by Kingston on the east. No doubt the Ontario Megalopolis eventually will stretch down the St. Lawrence River at least as far as Montreal, Quebec.

In the Midwest, parts of Indiana, Ohio, and Kentucky are rapidly growing together. The longitudinal axis extends from Indianapolis to Columbus, running through Richmond, Anderson, and Muncie in Indiana and through Dayton and Springfield in Ohio. The southward growth extends to Cincinnati and Covington and along the Ohio River southwestward to the Louisville area. The Indiana-Ohio-Kentucky Megalopolis is emerging as medium-sized industrial centers coalesce over an unusually fertile and productive agricultural landscape.

The Piedmont Megalopolis in the South is also developing on a rapidly contracting agricultural landscape, once a great cotton region. This urbanized area reaches from the vicinity of Atlanta, Georgia, northeastward through Greenville, South Carolina, and Charlotte, North Carolina, to the industrial ' cities of Winston-Salem, High Point, Greensboro, Durham, and Raleigh in North Carolina. One day this megalopolis will connect via southern Virginia with Gottman's Seaboard Megalopolis.

The Florida Megalopolis is perhaps the fastest growing in the country. In effect, it extends from Savannah, Georgia, southward along the entire Florida east coast to Miami. Almost halfway along the peninsula, in the vicinity of Orlando, this megalopolis crosses to Florida's west coast, where Tampa and St. Petersburg are the major centers. Virtually every county in Florida's peninsula gained population between 1960 and 1970 at a rate significantly faster than the thirteen percent growth rate for the United States as a whole; most of the counties grew by twenty-five percent or more.

A Gulf Coast Megalopolis is developing and threatening to stretch all the way from Mobile, Alabama, to Corpus Christi, Texas. At present, only a few gaps remain.

In California an extensive and complex megalopolis is taking shape, complementing the seaboard cities of the East. It begins at the Mexican border, where growth of the San Diego metropolis is dominant, and parallels the coast to the massive Los Angeles complex. The California Megalopolis then bifurcates north of Los Angeles, one branch following the Pacific coast through Santa Barbara and the other extending more directly northward through Bakersfield into the San Joaquin Valley. A thin strip of urban development continues along the coast to just north of San Francisco, and a wider swath on through the San Joaquin and Sacramento valleys to north of Sacramento. In the San Francisco and

Oakland area, these two arms of urban development merge once again to encircle San Francisco Bay, including the South Bay cities of San Mateo, Palo Alto, San Jose, Fremont, and Hayward.

Other scattered evidence exists of emerging megalopolises. The Washington-Oregon Megalopolis is extensive, though narrowly confined to the eastern side of Puget Sound (Seattle and Tacoma) and to the Willamette Valley (Portland to Eugene, Oregon). Considerable growth is also occurring along the eastern side of Great Salt Lake, including Ogden and Salt Lake City, south to Provo. Along the eastern side of the Front Range of the Colorado Rocky Mountains rapid urbanization is taking place, involving the outward growth of Denver and Colorado Springs. And finally, the Dallas-Fort Worth, Texas, system constitutes another emerging, though smaller, concentration of urbanization.

In sum, our oldest cities grew up because of ocean transport and the railroad. Later cities, such as San Diego, Denver, Houston, and Miami, have achieved metropolitan status because of the automobile. Our future cities, the spreading megalopolises, are developing as a result of electronic communication and the airplane. We are speedily moving away from the city as a concentration of population distinguishable from the countryside in the direction of the decentralized city which transforms the countryside into a continuous and extensive megalopolitan landscape. The growing need for information exchange compared to commodity exchange means the end of the traditional and compact city carrying out the transportation needs of a surrounding territory. The new urbanization can occur almost equally well anywhere, and thus favors pleasant climates or locations near, but not in, older centers. Communication technology, complementing electronics with personal travel, not only makes outward urban growth possible but also sets no particular limits on the extent of that growth. If the automobile began limited decentralization of cities, electronics has made possible almost unlimited decentralization.

The Role of Circulation in Planning the Urban Future

What are the implications of all of this urban spread for the art and science of planning. Where specifically does transportation and communication planning enter in? What are the relationships planners and policy makers need to be aware of between the alternatives of moving people among activities and of moving information among people? The efficient design of future metropolitan systems depends on the nature of the circulation taking place within each system and among all systems, and how the movement interlocks with the location of people and their activities.

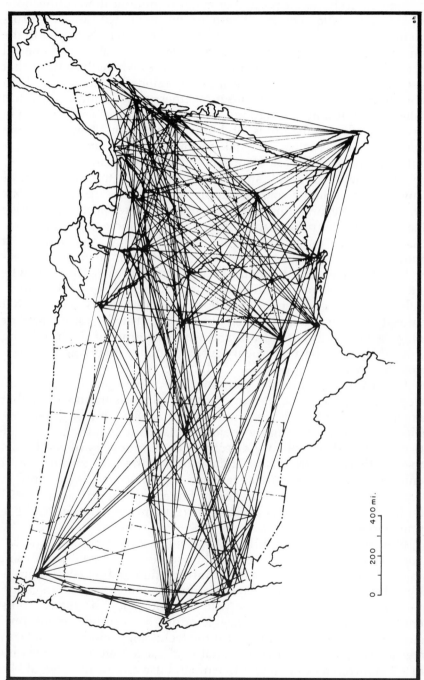

Figure 7.5: A theoretical pattern of communication linkages among U.S. metropolitan areas. The dense patterns of the East Coast and Midwest clearly reflect the existing and emerging megalopolises, and other linkages show the role of other major developing urbanized areas.

Figure 7.5 shows the pattern of major communication connections among U.S. population centers. These are the simulated flows of information invisibly crisscrossing the landscape. The pattern is similar to the pattern of air passenger movements, telephone calls, and postal deliveries. It shows the interaction between places where the cost of that interaction does not depend on distance. Functionally, the metropolitan areas of the country are coming closer together; and distance, which has controlled man's destiny throughout his evolutionary history, has been in part overcome for many kinds of human interaction. Nevertheless a strong need obviously remains for taking transportation and communication into account in all areas of urban and regional planning.

At the national level it should be realized that the advantages of scale and agglomeration economies apply only to cities up to about one million people.[5] Beyond this size, advantages, as revealed by average national growth rate, presumably do not result in increased agglomeration savings. The implications for national policy are that, in a communication-driven society in which concentration of people and activities has little advantage beyond a certain level, a greater effort must be made to establish urban growth centers in a variety of regional settings. The policy would encourage urbanization in medium to large centers that have already demonstrated the prerequisites for growth, not in small or declining centers. Going hand-in-hand with this type of decentralizing policy would have to be a rigorously enforced policy involving the internal growth and planning of these medium to large centers.

In treating this internal planning, look once again at Figure 7.2, the proposed neighborhood design. Its underlying assumptions are that movement will occur by private automobile, that heavy traffic generating activities will be located along the major arterials, and that the capacity of streets to move traffic will vary directly with the intensity of residential land use. Furthermore, the school and park are centrally located for travel convenience, and the commercial center is highly accessible not only to the neighborhood but also to other areas linked by two principal arterial streets. In this design there is an implicit relationship between land use and transportation.

Now imagine a quite different system of movement and interaction for this same area. Assume a highly sophisticated communication technology in which the movement of information and physical items is heavily substituted for the movement of people. Such a communication technology may not be a totally wild leap of fancy, as many of its elements are in whole or in part feasible or nearly so at the present time. Although this advanced communication technology might be able to operate superimposed on the traditional land use system represented by Figure 7.2, a different and more efficient land use arrangement would be preferred. As communications come to play an even larger role within

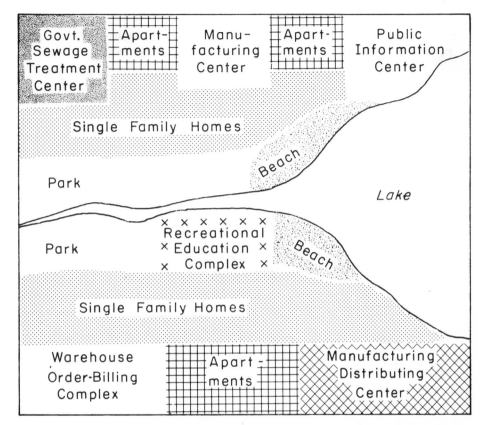

Figure 7.6:   An example of a land use, transportation, and communication pattern in a future neighborhood in which electronic communication plays a large role in human interaction.

our cities, as well as among them, planning and policy making will have to grapple with new prescriptions for urban design and function.

A new neighborhood layout to meet the assumptions of a communication-oriented urban society is depicted in Figure 7.6, a modification of the traditional land use and transportation plan described earlier. There is no single focus to this future neighborhood. Recreational and leisure-time activities occupy a larger proportion of neighborhood space. The neighborhood is delimited on three sides by facilities for the surface transport of people and of selected commodities shipped into and out of the neighborhood area. The sites of manufacturing-distributing and warehouse-storage facilities are thus in areas with maximum access to locations outside the neighborhood and in locations peripheral to the neighborhood itself. On the fourth side the neighborhood merges with a rather large artificial lake created by the damming of a stream.

Not obvious in Figure 7.6 are the vast networks of underground communication and commodity conduits linking homes and apartments. For example, the warehouse order-billing complex in the southwest corner is connected to each home and apartment by user-operated closed-circuit television. The operator at home is able to make his shopping selection over television, is automatically billed for his item selection, and has the product delivered via conduit within seconds. Likewise, the public information center disseminates cable television items, many of which may be dialed at the convenience of the viewer, and provides up-to-the-minute international, national and local news which is printed within seconds in an individual's home on teletype machines. The municipal sewage and solid waste center, a collection point for household sewage and all manner of solid wastes, has pipeline connections with each home and apartment unit for immediate sewage and garbage removal, processing, and recycling. Large proportions of the elementary and secondary education take place in the home with machine learning and individualized television feedback. The recreational-education complex near the center of the neighborhood provides primarily social and athletic outlets for children. Telephones with television hookups connect each home.

It is clear that a very different pattern of land use is possible when many kinds of movement and flow occur with the aid of electronics instead of individual auto, taxi, or transit trips. In the design of future metropolitan neighborhoods, therefore, certain features will need to be given increased policy attention. First of all leisure time will be enlarged for most individuals, and leisure-time activities will need to be provided at the neighborhood level. Although a high proportion of leisure activities will be available in the home, other kinds of activities, such as recreational swimming, boating, and picnicking, and entertainment, ought to be accessible within the neighborhood or relatively nearby. A present feature of cities is the lack of adequate recreational land within or near heavily populated areas. An inherent feature of recreational land is generally its non-intensive use. Many kinds of recreational activities are space-consumers — golf, tennis, picnicking, for example. Referring to our discussion of land values in Chapter 1, we recognize why golf courses are not found in downtown locations. In the future, however, it may prove desirable to have golf courses and other recreational, entertainment, and leisure activities more or less evenly grouped across the metropolitan landscape in response to the distribution of residential population.

A second and related factor to be recognized in planning future urban societies is that a different mix of locational factors will be involved in deciding where facilities and activities will be found. Specifically, the substitution of communication for transportation will mean only a greater footlooseness from the traditional factors of location. A whole group of new factors will emerge. A probable net effect of these factors will be more overall decentralization of the metropolitan system, but with continued clustering of specific elements within the diffused urban area. For example, recreational complexes, combining an appealing variety of experiences, will find obvious advantages in clustering. Industrial uses may also desire to cluster for reasons of material linkages or managerial overseeing.

The implication for planning is that sizable tracts of land in which an appropriate concentration of activity is focused must be available. At the present time, such sizable land areas, as for industrial parks, can be found only at the edge of the city. However, once a city has grown and spread into other cities to form a megalopolis, large land tracts will not be available unless especially created for future use. The urban sprawl so widely and often justifiably decried may be in this sense a blessing in disguise, since the scattering of urban development in peripheral areas does leave open land for future use. Policy decisions might well focus on ways of maintaining an adequate number of sufficiently large tracts for future integrated use.

A third consideration must be increasingly recognized by policy makers concerned with the future. That is the growing interdependence of locational decisions. Locating one facility at one selected place has a strong bearing on all future decisions to locate other facilities, whether of the same or different type. This locational interdependence of course has always existed but it has not always been recognized. It is especially critical for a megalopolitan system because, increasingly, emphasis must be given to making an existing pattern of urban land use function efficiently. When a city seems to be solving some of its problems by continual peripheral expansion, though at the expense of neglecting problems in the "old" part of the city, at least a large segment of the population is reasonably happy with urban, or rather suburban living. However, when suburbs stretch into suburbs over hundreds and hundreds of square miles, and there is no longer any "escape," locational choices made by one person or group will have to be seen as having implications for all concerned. Such a situation will necessitate a more direct and active role of governmental policy in putting forward, as well as resolving, locational planning.

Mass transit has been declining in importance for many years, and there seems little likelihood in the immediate future that it will again reach even its modest prominence of the past, unless major technological breakthroughs (e.g. antimagnetic locomotion) take place. Nevertheless, because of the necessity of maintaining activities in the central business district, mass transit must be continued, encouraged, and coordinated with auto transport. But apart from high-density transportation corridors serving a downtown destination, and specific projects in specific cities, the future of mass transit as a whole is not bright. It will remain most evident in older American cities having a high density of people and activities. Although we will continue to hear a great deal in the public media about new transit experiments and developments, transit will probably occupy a rather minor role in the overall circulation of most cities. New technological breakthroughs may somewhat reduce the dependency of transit on high-density routes, but transit does not seem to be the trend, at least in the near and intermediate future. Experiments in free transit have not encouraged many citizens to abandon their automobiles.

The automobile will continue to transform our cities and be the major form of internal movement of people. Because it was the automobile that decentralized cities, it is only the automobile that is able to maintain that decentralization, with an added boost from communication technology. In the future, the auto may take on new features and be propelled by different forms of power, such as turbine, steam, or electric motors. But it will still be the private auto, in some form. One likely development will be some type of automatic guidance and control along selected routes, both inter- and intracity. The vehicle would have two sets of controls, one for manual guidance along low density street systems and one linked to a computer controlled, non-driver system along high density arteries.

If the automobile represents not only the present but also the probable future trend in internal circulation in cities, there are several profound implications for the urban environment and for urban planning. The most salient at the present is the social cost of atmospheric pollution. The internal combustion engine has been developed to give reliable performance economically. The combustion process in the past was regarded as satisfactory if the engines operated at reasonable speeds, with quick acceleration, without engine "knock" or undue wear, and with consistency. When automobiles were rare and when there was no particular geographic concentration of them, the problems of waste products did not seem very important. Today automobile pollution is recognized as a severe problem in large and small cities alike.

The people of the United States and Canada have become strongly concentrated in urban areas. So have their automobiles. This concentration results in serious outpourings of a variety of pollutants in locations where the most damage can be done to the greatest number of people. In 1970 there were 108 million motor vehicles registered in the United States, nearly one-half the world total. These vehicles annually emitted approximately 80 million tons of pollutants, or about three-quarters of a ton each. Most pedestrians on downtown city streets are aware of the odor of auto exhaust and of the heavy pollutants in the air, but few people seem to realize the extent to which they themselves contribute to auto emissions. If these waste products were somehow trapped in a hypothetical auto "waste basket" and had to be manually removed each day, auto users would very quickly grasp the extent and significance of vehicle pollution. Instead, pollutants escape into the air where they spread widely and affect the entire population.

Automobile pollution not only results from tailpipe emissions, but also from evaporation from gas tanks and carburetors and from crankcase blowby. Roughly three million tons of hydrocarbons enter the atmosphere each year through gasoline evaporation alone. Between one-quarter and one-third of auto exhaust is vented from a tube extending from the crankcase. This crankcase blowby results from imperfectly combusted fuel getting past the pistons along the cylinder walls and entering the crankcase. Unburned or partially burned hydrocarbons are emitted. The major outpouring of waste products, however, takes place through the tailpipe. Here not only are incompletely combusted hydrocarbons released into the air, but carbon dioxide, carbon monoxide, nitrogen dioxide, sulphur oxides, lead, and particulate matter are as well. The automobile is the single greatest source of carbon monoxide, hydrocarbons, and nitrogen oxides. Estimates are that generally nearly one-half of all air pollution produced in the United States and Canada is from motor vehicles.

Air transportation must also be considered in any discussion of future urban societies. The movement of people and cargo by air has been growing at a phenomenal rate and is already exerting a notable effect on the growth and development of cities. The major metropolitan airport not only occupies a large segment of land area but also has an influence on surrounding land uses. Industry increasingly realizes the advantage of a location with high access to a large airport, not only for ease of personnel mobility but also for receiving and shipping "emergency" items needed on almost instant notice to avoid breakdown or delay. The airport has already far exceeded the old railroad station in importance and influence. In the future city, the major airport will need to be more fully recognized as a fundamental organizational center on which many kinds of activities and individuals will focus. Planners must be in a position to help resolve locational conflicts which emerge from competition and resulting congestion around major airport facilities. As national and international mobility becomes even more commonplace, the airport and its surrounding and supporting facilities will become one of the most dominant features of the urban area and one of the few features giving focus to the otherwise ever-spreading urbanization process.

If we are going to combine future growth with a better urban environment, we must be willing to pay the cost. Today one is encouraged to pollute the air with his automobile, for example, because his private benefits outweigh private costs. Social costs are incurred by society as a whole because of an individual's activities, the cost of which he does not fully bear. We should turn the entire situation around and generate a system of social benefits, not social costs. Social benefits would thus be advantages enjoyed by society as a result of private actions which do not yield direct benefits to the individual. Mere recognition of such social benefits is often enough to lead to their realization, as psychological benefits to the individual may be encouraged through education and understanding. Awareness that one is destroying the world around him is a strong stimulus, though not always sufficient, to change behavior. We have to learn to live within the constraints of our present environment as we plan for the better cities of the future. Although our transportation system imposes social costs on our cities, it has also provided great social benefits. We need to harness our urban transportation environment and harmonize its positive and negative energies in the direction of a socially pleasant and rewarding life in the city of the future.

References

1. Roger Creighton, *Urban Transportation Planning* (Urbana: University of Illinois Press, 1970).
2. Harold Brodsky, "Land Development and the Expanding City," *Annals of the Association of American Geographers*, Vol. 63, June, 1973, pp. 159 - 166.
3. Jean Gottmann, *Megalopolis: The Urbanized Northeastern Seaboard of the United States* (Cambridge: M.I.T. Press, 1961).
4. See John R. Brochert, "America's Changing Metropolitan Regions," *Annals of the Association of American Geographers*, Vol. 62, June, 1972, pp. 352 - 373.
5. Brian J.L. Berry, "Contemporary Urbanization Processes," in Frank E. Horton, editor, *Geographical Perspectives and Urban Problems* (Washington, D.C.: National Academy of Sciences, 1973), pp. 94 - 107.
6. Richard H. Wagner, *Environment and Man* (New York: Norton & Company, 1971), pp. 170 - 195.

Chapter 8

Summary Review

It has been the intention of these pages to show that circulation is a vital part of the urban scene. Emphasis has been placed on human movement, i.e., flows of people and of information, ideas, and communications in the city. Human movement has an influence on the whole range of features associated with urban living. Locational decisions involving people and activities in the city must operate within the parameters of the circulation system.

Urbanization has placed a tremendous strain on societal relationships and cultural traditions. Throughout most of man's evolutionary history, he existed within small and closely knit social units which were not only powerful checks on deviant behavior, as determined within the particular unit, but were also basic in engendering a sense of belonging and identity. Each individual had a recognized role and place within the community. Central to the community identity was some type of family or kinship structure, which fostered close social ties and a sense of well-being. Furthermore, the social units existed within a bounded geographic space, proximity being an added incentive to maintaining group social cohesion. Social ties, including kinship, were the primary factor determining one's choice of where to live.

With the development of the city and its necessary employment conditions, the workplace became the single most important influence on the decision of where to live. Jobs began to pull people away from their traditional social and familial units, and economic rather than social factors became paramount. Migration to employment centers fragmented the family geographically and socioeconomically, though lingering elements of the old social order have remained and continue to exert some influence on the new lifestyle; migration decisions, for example, are often made on the information of relatives who know about employment opportunities.

Many of the frictions and frustrations of urban living have to do with establishing a satisfactory set of social relationships. The search for a social equilibrium reminiscent of ancient social and kinship groups lies at the core of the way man has molded his cities. In fact, this search may well account, more than is generally realized, for the restless migratory nature of urban households. Yet urbanization, by the very nature of its economic spawning, has been in many ways incompatible with a social equilibrium. A number of devices have been created to bring social unity into the urban setting.

One of the most obvious is the urban neighborhood, a confined geographic collection of residential and other land uses. As we have seen, however, the neighborhood has proven to be an imperfect social unit. It is a collection of individuals, perhaps somewhat alike in socioeconomic status, but varied in experience and sharing no essential bond or identity. Households come and go in a neighborhood. Proximity seeks to supplant blood bonds or permanently and mutually acknowledged social commitments. Social ties, such as they are, typically extend far away from the geographic neighborhood. We find residential change increasingly characterizing urbanized society — so much so that fewer and fewer individuals can identify with a place called home. With the tremendous growth in popularity of apartment dwelling, a sizable segment of society have come to accept their transitory role in a particular apartment complex and in a transitory society.

A number of cultural elements enter into the development of urban neighborhoods to make them, in a limited and wholly negative sense, a substitute for the pre-urban social order. That of racial attitudes is the most noticeable in our present cities. The racially-inspired flight of whites into the surrounding suburbs and countryside has produced the ghetto, a concentration of black neighborhoods located usually in the older portions of the urban area. Different cultural elements characterize the black and white populations of the cities, and alarmingly little social interaction occurs between the two groups. Just as the small social units of the past identified with their own members and distinguished them from those outside the group, so too has black-white society taken up a within-without group attitude that fundamentally affects the entire social fabric of the city.

Were it not for the ease of movement of people, commodities, and information, cities could not exist as they do today. Circulation permits our urban society to function, but it also has accelerated societal fragmentation by allowing people to live and work increasingly far apart. When the friction of movement was high, the individual was forced to work near his place of residence. As the time, effort, and cost of getting to work decreased, he had a greater choice of where to live in the city. His residential choice came to rest more on amenity-related factors than on proximity to work. As longer work-trips characterized more and more people, growing traffic congestion was the inevitable result. For many groups, particularly lower-income families, the shift of employment away from the downtown further exacerbated the problem of getting to work.

The city has become composed of growing numbers of socially uprooted individuals and families, pulled one way by a desire to establish and maintain new social relations based on past patterns and propelled in another direction by economic factors frequently demanding transitory and superficial social ties. However, at the same time the sheer number of people confined in a bounded geographic space has meant an increase in social opportunities for any one individual or family.

Part of the problem in maintaining long distance social ties has been alleviated by the growing importance of communication technology. Not only social ties but also many other kinds of human interaction rely on electronic communications as a substitute for person-to-person exchanges. Even so, communication technology has not proven fully adequate to re-establish the equilibrium of traditional social relationships. Human socialization remains a sufficiently subtle process that it can meaningfully occur only on a face-to-face basis, although the ease of maintaining social relations may be aided by electronic means.

Drawing heavily upon the increased speed and volume of information exchange possible within and between cities is a long list of institutions, industries, organizations, and service agencies. These activities have become information-oriented and are drawn to cities because of information access and storage advantages found there. Metropolitan areas have always had an important employment function, being a place where workers and jobs were concentrated. With the rise of a communication society, a reinforcement in the role of the urban job market has occurred, but with a tremendous increase in the number of jobs which involve in some way information handling or manipulating.

It is thus a paradox that the urban society is in a state of social imbalance, in contrast to the traditional agrarian society for example, since a fundamental purpose of urban areas is to maximize the opportunity for contacts among people. Urban society on the whole has been slow to capitalize on the social advantages human agglomeration provides. Cities, which developed largely so that people could be near activities, need to find better ways of getting people nearer to people. To do so goes well beyond the provision of new transportation facilities or communication innovations, as it involves reducing social distance, racial distance, and psychological distance.

In planning a better life in our cities, greater attention must be placed on the organization of space in which human movement occurs

and the consequences of this spatial organization for the location of activities and people in cities. Since the nature of linkages between places
fundamentally affects the activities occurring at those places, circulation
policy is basic to the fabric of urban life. New transportation and communication facilities must connect actual places and thus have a spatial
expression on the urban landscape which affects people and activities in
the city differently. What is an advantage to an activity located at one
place will become a disadvantage to the same kind of activity located
elsewhere when a transport route, for example, changes the pattern of
accessibility. Likewise, individuals residing in different locations will
react differently, depending on how their patterns of accessibility are
altered. If these changes are to promote a better life in the city of the
future, human beings, not facilities, must be the first priority of urban
transportation planning.

It is crucial that the future problems of the city be dealt with in a
manner both orderly and imaginative. The city must not be viewed as an
insurmountable barrier to a high quality of life, but rather as a vehicle
which, if guided properly, can carry man to a higher level of social
organization. The multitudes of individual decisions that have directed
the growth of the city in the past must be replaced by truly comprehensive planning. And the expanding technology of circulation must be
harnessed to meet the needs of our expanding cities.

Since the time of the Industrial Revolution cities have changed in
response to technology operating within, and driven by, the economic
system. Thus our present cities are the artifacts of past technologies in
conflict with future possibilities. The social organization of cities first
disrupted the tightly bound social system of the past, and then itself has
undergone continuous alteration and readjustment as new technology
has made possible new social organization. Central in its impact on
changing the urban social system has been the technology of transportation and, more recently, communication.

We spoke in Chapter 7 of three phases of clustered human
settlement: the small, compact settlement (village); the spatially confined
city; and the rapidly spreading megalopolis. We might also speak of three
corresponding phases of human social organization: the spatially prox-
imate and temporally stable kinship-related system composed of relatively few members; the temporally unstable organization based in large part
on the urban "neighborhood" (an imperfect carry over of spatial proximity); and the emergent social system driven by communication
technology and information exchange, spatially diffused nationally and
even internationally. The latter system of social organization presently
involves a limited but rapidly growing number of individuals, with high
income levels, whose local or even metropolitan identification has been
almost entirely replaced by loyalty and identification with some regional,

national, or international institution or organization. Such institutions exist for a wide variety of purposes, from profit-seeking in the case of corporations to good deeds in philanthropic and religious groups to truth seeking in scientific and research organizations. These organizations, with their own conditions of entry, loyalty monitoring, status rewards, and even welfare systems, act fundamentally as social organizations with which an individual can identify and achieve a sense of belonging. In this sense they are relatively stable and come amazingly close to fulfilling the functions of the older kinship, tribal, and village social order.

Significantly, these organizations most typically comprise spatially diffused members. Loyalty and affinity are immediately and mutually recognized by the members, as it is the concept of the organization with its goals and problems that attracts and holds the membership. In the developing megalopolitan systems, already engulfing large segments of North America, growing numbers of individuals are attaching themselves to one type of organization or another, most frequently via their employment or profession. In all cases, these organizations are information-oriented, and the person-to-person exchange of information, whether direct or indirect (as through the printed word), acts as a medium for social interaction.

Consider the case of a shoe manufacturer. He has evolved his own trade jargon intelligible to those in the same business, much as a dialect served in the past to differentiate tribe from tribe. His business associations are with those in the shoe industry, and the wider his associations the broader his knowledge of impending style changes, cost conditions, and pricing and sales possibilities. Because his business activities consume most of his energy, his business and social contacts largely overlap. This is not to say that our shoe manufacturer does not play other roles, as parent, husband, or lawnkeeper; or function in other organizations by being a civic leader, church goer, or country club member. He perceives his loyalties, however, to belong principally to the community of business associates engaged in a common enterprise and having a common welfare.

Herein lie some long-term implications for social planning and policy. Individuals such as our shoe manufacturer, who have national business and social communication networks, less frequently identify with local issues and problems. Their personal perspective is more national or intermetropolitan in focus, implying that the solution to many metropolitan problems may also be national, rather than local as has heretofore been thought. Metropolitan planners must develop policies and design plans in tune with the prevailing technological trends — which is to say within the probable capabilities of the transportation and communication systems presently evolving. Since the future metropolitan complex will be national in character, though retaining local characteristics, much of the effort to improve the life quality of the future urban environment must be predicated upon technological change that inevitably will have national impact.

Selected Bibliography

1. Abler, Ronald F., "Distance, Intercommunications and Geography," *Proceedings, Association of American Geographers*, Vol. 3 (1971), pp. 28 - 31.

2. Abler, Ronald F., et al, *Spatial Organization: The Geographer's View of the World*, Englewood Cliffs, N.Y.: Prentice-Hall, 1971.

3. Appleton, J.H., *The Geography of Communications in Great Britain*, London: Oxford University Press, 1962.

4. Banfield, Edward C., *The Unheavenly City*, Boston: Little, Brown and Company, 1970.

5. Berry, Brian J. L., "The Geography of the United States in the Year 2000," *Ekistics*, Vol. 29 (1970), pp. 339 - 351.

6. Black, William R., "Trip Distribution and Urban Spatial Behavior," *East Lakes Geographer*, Vol. 7 (1971), pp. 13 - 21.

7. Buchanan, Colin, *Traffic in Towns: A Study of the Long Term Problems of Traffic in Urban Areas*, London: Her Majesty's Stationery Office, 1963.

8. Chapin, F. Stuart, Jr., *Urban Land Use Planning*, Urbana: University of Illinois Press, 1965.

9. Clark, Colin, "Transport: Maker and Breaker of Cities," *Town Planning Review*, Vol. 28 (1958), pp. 237 - 250.

10. Chinitz, Benjamin, *Freight and the Metropolis*, Cambridge: Harvard University Press, 1960.

11. Creighton, Roger L., *Urban Transportation Planning*, Urbana: University of Illinois Press, 1970.

12. Doxiadis, Constantinos A., *Ekistics: An Introduction to the Science of Human Settlements*, New York: Oxford University Press, 1968.

13. Duhl, Leonard J., and John Powell, (eds.), *The Urban Condition: People and Policy in the Metropolis*, New York: Basic Books, Inc., 1971.

14. Dyckman, John, "Transportation in Cities," *Scientific American*, Vol. 213 (1965), pp. 162 - 174.

15. Epps, Richard W., "Suburban Jobs and Black Workers," *Business Review: Philadelphia Federal Reserve Bank*, (1969), pp. 3 - 13.

16. Gilmore, Harlan W., *Transportation and the Growth of Cities*, Glencoe, Illinois: The Free Press, 1963.

17. Gottman, Jean, *Megalopolis: The Urbanized Northeastern Seaboard of the United States*, Cambridge: M.I.T. Press, 1964.

18. Hall, Edward T., *The Hidden Dimension*, Garden City: Doubleday and Co., Inc., 1969.

19. Hay, William W., *An Introduction to Transportation Engineering*, New York: John Wiley and Sons, Inc., 1965.

20. Horton, Frank (ed.), *Geographic Studies of Urban Transportation and Network Analysis*, Department of Geography, Study No. 16, Evanston: Northwestern University, 1968.

21. Horton, Frank, and David R. Reynolds, "Effects of Urban Spatial Structure on Individual Behavior," *Economic Geography*, Vol. 47 (1971), pp. 36 - 48.

22. Jefferson, Mark, "The Civilizing Rails," *Economic Geography*, Vol. 4 (1928), pp. 217 - 231.

23. Lynch, Kevin, *The Image of the City*, Cambridge: The M.I.T. Press, 1960.

24. MacKay, W.K. and J.C. Latchford, "Transportation and Land Use Structures," *Urban Studies*, Vol. 4 (1967), pp. 201 - 217.

25. Mayer, Harold M., "Cities: Transportation and Internal Circulation," *Journal of Geography*, Vol. 68 (1969), pp. 390 - 405.

26. Mayer, Harold M., "Urban Geography and Urban Transportation Planning," *Traffic Quarterly*, Vol. 17 (1963), pp. 610 - 631.

27. Meier, Richard L., *A Communications Theory of Urban Growth*, Cambridge: The M.I.T. Press, 1962.

28. Mitchell, Robert B., and Chester Rapkin, *Urban Traffic: A Function of Land Use*, New York: Columbia University Press; 1954.

29. Mumford, Lewis, *The Highway and the City*, New York: Harcourt, Brace and World, Inc.; 1963.

30. Owen, Wilfred, *The Metropolitan Transportation Problem*, rev. ed., Washington: Brookings Institution, 1966.

31. Owen, Wilfred, *The Accessible City*, Washington: Brookings Institution, 1972.

32. Pred, Allan R., *The Spatial Dynamics of U.S. Urban-Industrial Growth, 1800-1914*, The Regional Science Studies Series, Cambridge: The M.I.T. Press, 1966.

33. Pred, Allan R., "Urban Systems Development and the Long Distance Flow of Information Through Pre-electronic U.S. Newspapers," *Economic Geography*, Vol. 47 (1971), pp. 498 - 524.

34. Reisch, Diana, *Problems of Mass Transportation*, New York: H.W. Wilson Co., 1970.

35. Smerk, George M., *Urban Transportation: The Federal Role*, Bloomington: Indiana University Press, 1965.

36. Smerk, George M., *Readings in Urban Transportation*, Bloomington: Indiana University Press, 1968.

37. Spreiregen, Paul D., ed., *The Modern Metropolis: Its Origins, Growth, Characteristics, and Planning*, Cambridge: The M.I.T. Press, 1967.

38. Taaffe, Edward J., et al., *The Peripheral Journey to Work*, Evanston: Northwestern University Press, 1963.

39. Taaffe, Edward J., "The Transportation Network and the Changing American Landscape," in *Problems and Trends in American Geography*, ed., Saul B. Cohen, New York: Basic Books, 1967, 15 - 25.

40. Taaffe, Edward J., and Howard L. Gauthier, *Geography of Transportation*, Englewood Cliffs, N.J.: Prentice-Hall, 1973.

41. Thompson, Wilbur, *A Preface to Urban Economics*, Baltimore: The Johns Hopkins Press, 1968.

42. Toffler, Alvin, *Future Shock*, New York: Bantam Books, Inc. 1971.

43. Ullman, Edward L., "The Role of Transportation and the Bases for Interaction," in *Man's Role in Changing the Face of the Earth*, ed. William L. Thomas, Jr., Chicago: The University of Chicago Press, 1956.

44. Von Eckardt, Wolf, *A Place to Live*, New York: Delacorte Press, 1967.

Index